THE
INTERNATIONAL
CUISINES
CALORIE COUNTER

DENSIE WEBB
Ph.D., R.D.

M. EVANS AND COMPANY, NEW YORK

Library of Congress Cataloging-in-Publication Data

Webb, Densie.
The international cuisines calorie counter / Densie Webb.
p.   cm.
Includes bibliographical references.
ISBN 0-87131-593-9
1. Food—Calorie content—Tables. 2. Cookery, International.
I. Title
TX551.W4   1990   89-77267
641.1'042—dc20

M. Evans and Company, Inc.
216 East 49 Street
New York, New York 10017

MANUFACTURED IN THE UNITED STATES OF AMERICA

2 4 6 8 9 7 5 3 1

CONTENTS

INTRODUCTION

Eating ethnic is in. The question today is not where you want to eat but which country's cuisine you crave. Mexican, Italian, and Chinese are the uncontested favorites across the United States, but other cuisines such as Indian, Japanese, and Cajun are rapidly gaining popularity.

Trying dishes full of new aromas and new flavors is a pleasure, but it can also mean venturing into unfamiliar terrain when you're trying to eat a healthful diet. However, no cuisine need be taboo. It's simply a matter of knowing which dishes are the best bets. That's the reason this book was developed—to help you make healthful eating decisions, whether you're eating take-out Chinese or sitting down to an elegant seven-course French dinner.

As you thumb through these pages, some surprises

are in store. For example, did you know that despite their reputation for being low in fat and low in calories, many Chinese dishes are deep-fried and *then* stir-fried? Or that Cajun cuisine has one of the highest fat levels and that serving sizes can only be described as gargantuan? Or that more traditional Mexican food uses lard (loaded with saturated fat and cholesterol—both bad for your heart) while the *nuevo* Mexican establishments tend to use more heart-healthy vegetable oil?

Each ethnic cuisine has its own "secrets" that range from hidden fat in its dishes to often-overlooked but wonderfully low-calorie choices. This book provides a few of these secrets, including the calorie and fat content and basic ingredients of foods for fifteen international cuisines. In addition, specific tips and a list of Best Bets for each cuisine—that is, the dishes that have the lowest percentage of calories from fat—are given. The Best Bets provided at the beginning of each section are not, however, the only good choices. Just because the percentage of calories from fat in a dish is high doesn't necessarily mean the total fat is too high. For example, if a small amount of butter is added to low-fat broccoli, then the percentage of calories from fat of the dish would be high, since broccoli contributes little to the total calorie count. When choosing your own best bets, be sure to look at both the total-fat and the percent-calories-as-fat columns.

Also keep in mind that ingredients, as well as serving sizes, vary tremendously from recipe to recipe and from one restaurant to another. The recipe for Enchiladas Rancheras that your favorite Mexican restaurant uses, for example, may be quite different from the recipe used for the calculations in this book, and therefore the calorie and fat content may differ as well. Even so, the Guide is an invaluable resource that lets you know how foods are generally prepared and which ones tend to be lowest in fat and calories. Of course, if you decide to prepare these dishes at home using the same cookbooks used to make this guide's calorie calculations (listed in Reference Section), you'll know precisely the number of calories and the amount of fat you're getting. Obviously, not all of the world's cuisines are presented in this book. But the fifteen cuisines chosen represent the ones most familiar to us in the United States, arranged in order of their popularity.

TIPS FOR EATING ETHNIC IN RESTAURANTS

Regardless of which cuisine you choose, healthful eating should be your goal. If you're cooking at home, lowering the fat and calories in an ethnic recipe is easy because you're in control. (See "Tips for Eating Ethnic at Home," below.) In restaurants, someone else is doing the cooking and you must be vigilant in your quest for healthful dishes. Follow the strategies provided below, and any country's cuisine can become part of your low-fat, low-calorie eating plan.

• *Phone ahead.* If possible, call the restaurant ahead of time and ask if they will prepare dishes to order, e.g., Filet of Sole without the butter or Pasta with Garlic and Oil with half the oil. Also find out if there is an extra charge for you and your dining partner to share an entree. Sharing is an excellent way of removing the temptation to consume more than you really need. If you're concerned about sodium, ask if your dish can be prepared without it.

- *Ask Questions.* Once you get the menu, ask the waiter about how specific dishes are prepared. Is it marinated in oil before grilling? Is it stir-fried or deep-fried or both? Is the meat lean? Is it topped with cream, sour cream, or cheese? Be forewarned that waiters don't always have the answers to your questions. After all, they are waiters, not chefs. But be assertive. Ask if the waiter would please ask your questions of the person preparing the food. In ethnic restaurants you may have the added challenge of communicating with waiters who speak little English. And more expensive ethnic restaurants may not provide English translations on their menus. If that's the case, you have no choice but to ask.

- *Be Creative.* If there are no acceptable entrees on the menu, try the appetizers, salads, and side dishes. You may find wonderful choices with which to create your own meal. Steamed mussels (without butter dip), green salad (with dressing on the side), onion soup (without cheese), or shrimp cocktail are all good choices usually found outside the entree list.

- *Know the Lingo.* Being familiar with cooking terms puts you one step ahead of the game. Knowing which terms mean fat is lurking in your food makes it possible to narrow down the choices yourself before asking the waiter more specific questions. For example, sauteed, creamy, sauce, thick, marbled, flaky, crispy, breaded, batter-dipped—all mean that fat (butter, lard, margarine, or oil) was used in preparation. The terms to look for are: steamed, broiled, poached, grilled, roasted, in its own juice. But make sure the description is accurate. For example, Chinese "smoked" fish may actually be deep-fried.

- *Take a Menu Home.* This allows you to take as much time as you need to look over the menu and make the most healthful eating decisions. It may, however, be practical only in less expensive eating establishments. In higher-priced restaurants, the menus are likely to be costly themselves and owners are understandably reluctant to hand them out free of charge. In large cities, restaurant guides are commonly found in local book stores. The guides often include copies of actual menus or at least a sampling of what each restaurant has to offer. It's money well spent if it helps you avoid dieting disasters when eating out.

- *Share.* It's the best and easiest way to cut calories. Share a dish of Peking Duck and you automatically cut the calories from 773 per serving to 386 (although the percentage of calories from fat is still high—67 percent.)

TIPS FOR EATING ETHNIC AT HOME

If you're cooking at home, there are several ways that you can trim the fat and cut the calories from the original recipes. Purists will say you're ruining the true flavor of the cuisine, but it's really the wide variety of herbs and spices that should offer your taste buds a break from your usual eating routine, not the added fat. The three basic principles for modifying recipes are reduction, substitution, and elimination—reduce the amount of fattening ingredients, substitute lower-calorie ingredients where possible, and eliminate fattening ingredients that are not essential.

- When cooking meats, drain off excess fat before adding other ingredients to the pan.

- Steam vegetables and season them with spices rather than smothering them in butter.

- Cut in half the butter or oil that recipes call for.

- If you must pan-fry or deep-fry, make sure the oil is hot before using it. The hotter the oil, the less oil the food will absorb during frying.

- When possible, cook stews, soups, sauces, and gravies ahead of time, refrigerate, and skim off the congealed fat before using.

- Buy lean cuts and grades of meats and trim off all visible fat. Use a tenderizing marinade containing vinegar, tomato juice, lemon juice, or wine rather than opting for fattier cuts of meat.

- Use low-calorie mayonnaise and sour cream substitutes when possible. But be careful when substituting low-calorie margarines. They contain more water than regular margarine and will change the character of the dish.

- Make serving sizes smaller than the recipe calls for. For example, some recipes (Cajun, in particular) say they are for four people, when they are actually more than enough for eight.

- Use evaporated skim milk or low-fat milk in recipes that call for cream or half-and-half.

- Try a reduced-fat cheese instead of the real thing. Like low-calorie margarines, they contain more water than the original version, so you may have to experiment to find out which one gives you the best results.

- In recipes for baked foods, reduce the fat and sugar by one-third. If the dish looks and tastes fine, take it one step further and try cutting a little more next time.

RECOMMENDATIONS FOR HEALTHFUL EATING

C a l o r i e s Your exact calorie requirements depend on several factors, including your sex, age, weight, how much you exercise, what percentage of your body weight is fat or muscle, whether or not you've been dieting recently, and whether or not you smoke. Unfortunately, there is no easy way to figure in all these factors and calculate the exact number of calories you need to lose weight or at least head off weight gain. If you're a longtime calorie counter, you probably know your own calorie limits from experience. But generally speaking, women usually require 1400 to 2500 calories per day to maintain their weight; men 2000 to 3300 per day. If you're trying to lose weight, the important thing to know is that you must eat fewer calories. But say, for example, that you've decided to cut back to 1500 calories per day. You obviously would have no room for a 1096-calorie serving of the Cajun soup Boulli with Rice, but a 257-calorie half-serving of Shrimp and Crabmeat Jambalaya (see Cajun Food Section) would fit nicely into your low-calorie diet plan.

F a t Another important point about calories: Nutritionists used to believe that "a calorie is a calorie," but not anymore. In the last few years research has revealed that, calorie for calorie, fatty foods may lay down more body fat than do carbohydrates (including sugar) or protein. Most major health organizations recommend that you keep the fat in your diet to 30 percent or less of your total day's calories. But some nutritionists recommend that to lose weight you need to keep it to 20 to 25 percent of calories. That figures out to be about 2 to 3 grams of fat per 100 calories you consume. The chart below shows how much fat you can allow yourself and still be within healthy limits.

If your total daily calories are:	Then eat no more than:
1000	33 grams of fat
1200	40 grams of fat
1500	50 grams of fat
1800	60 grams of fat
2100	70 grams of fat
2400	80 grams of fat
2700	90 grams of fat

There is a difference in fats when it comes to being heart-healthy. Polyunsaturated and monounsaturated fats such as safflower, canola, soybean, corn, peanut, and olive oils are better for controlling the level of cholesterol in your blood than are saturated fats like butter and lard (which contain cholesterol). In this book, the ingredients listed after each dish reveal if fat is an ingredient, but you'll have to ask at your restaurant to find out what type of fat they use.

Cholesterol The American Heart Association and the National Cholesterol Education Program recommend that you restrict your cholesterol intake to less than 300 milligrams per day. Cholesterol counts for international dishes aren't provided in this guide because of the variability in the fats that restaurants use. If a restaurant substitutes any one of the vegetable oils for lard, the cholesterol count drops from 12 milligrams per tablespoon to zero; if vegetable oil replaces butter it drops from 30 milligrams to zero. Another important point: Don't confuse "healthful" with "low-calorie." Safflower oil may be better for your arteries than lard, but they both offer approximately 120 calories per tablespoon.

Sugar While there's nothing particularly unhealthy about sugar (except that it causes cavities), it is devoid of vitamins and minerals and provides only calories. For this reason alone, you should keep sugar to a minimum in your diet. Don't think that other sweeteners such as honey, corn syrup, or brown sugar are more nutritious. The amounts of vitamins and minerals that honey and brown sugar contain are insignificant, and your body still uses them as sugars as it does white sugar.

Sodium The amount of salt used in cooking probably varies more than any other ingredient. For that reason, no information on the sodium content of international dishes is provided in this guide. Your best strategy is to ask that no sodium be added in preparing your meal and to add no salt at the table. The National Research Council of the National Academy of Sciences says that 1100–3300 milligrams a day is a safe and adequate intake of sodium.

The calculations in this book were made using the recipes from a variety of ethnic cookbooks (see Appendix). The recipes were analyzed for their calorie and fat content using CBORD's Diet Analyzer computer program with ESHA nutrient data base and Nutritionist III. Calorie counts for food items missing from the data bases were obtained from the USDA Handbook 8, Jean A. T. Pennington and Helen Nichols Church's *Food Values of Portions Commonly Used,* 1985, the USDA Handbook 456, and from specific product information. Appropriate substitutions were made for ingredients where nutrient information was not available.

Figures for grams of fat were rounded to the nearest whole number. Percent calories from fat figures were calculated using grams of fat before rounding. This calculated percentage was then rounded to the nearest whole number.

Very little data is available on how much fat is absorbed during deep-fat frying. For foods that are deep-fried, estimates of fat absorption were made and used consistently with all recipes. Most dishes were calculated on a per-serving basis as suggested by the recipe. Some dishes were calculated with side dishes such as rice or noodles included, if they are an integral part of the dish. Others were not. For example, rice was not included in the calculations for most Chinese dishes, but it was included for several Cajun dishes. If you always eat rice with your Chinese food, be sure to add the calories from the rice to get the true calorie total.

CHINESE FOOD

Despite Chinese food's reputation for being low-calorie, many Chinese dishes are high in fat because they are stir-fried, deep-fried, or both. The amount of oil used in stir-frying varies from a single tablespoon in a recipe to four or five tablespoons. At 120 calories per tablespoon you can see how quickly the calories add up. Since stir-frying is the traditional way to prepare Chinese food you can't avoid fat, but you can stay away from deep-fried dishes. Be sure to ask if a dish is deep-fried because the names can be misleading. For example, Lemon Chicken and Smoked Fish, which sound low-fat, are actually deep-fried. On the other hand, a few dishes are good choices, even though they contain more than the recommended 30 percent of calories from fat. Snow Peas, Water Chestnuts, and Bamboo Shoots is a dish that is low in total calories and fat. But because the main ingredients are low in calories, most of the calories (54 percent) come from the small amount of oil used in stir-frying the dish.

Regardless of which entree you decide on, allow yourself a generous portion of steamed rice with a relatively small portion of the entree. Chinese soups are a good low-fat way to start your meal and curb your appetite. But even here there are exceptions, like Sizzling Rice Soup, which is made with fried rice. If you're concerned about sodium, remember that soy sauce is extremely high in sodium (1029 milligrams per tablespoon). Duck sauce and plum sauce—condiments usually set on the table—are okay if you use them in small amounts. They are equivalent to using jam or jelly, but they are fat-free. The dishes listed below are low in fat.

CHINESE BEST BETS

Chicken Wonton Soup • *Drunken Chicken* • *Hot and Sour Soup* • *Mandarin Pancakes* • *Peking Smoked Chicken* • *Subgum Soup* • *Velvet Chicken Lo Mein* • *Velvet Corn Soup with Crabmeat*

CHINESE	Calories per serving	Fat (Grams)	% Calories as fat
Asparagus in Crabmeat Sauce (Rice not included) Asparagus, broth, cornstarch, sherry, egg whites, crabmeat, oil, sugar	148	10	63
Bean Curd with Shredded Pork (Rice not included) Pork, bean curd, mushrooms, soy sauce, broth, sherry, cornstarch	198	16	73
Bean Sprouts with Chicken Shreds and Almonds (Rice not included) Chicken, almonds, mushrooms, cornstarch, soy sauce, sherry, oil, onions, sugar, bean sprouts, bell peppers	317	20	56
Beef with Broccoli (Rice not included) Steak, broccoli, sherry, cornstarch, oil, sugar	596	39	59

CHINESE	Calories per serving	Fat (Grams)	% Calories as fat
Beef with Peppers (Rice not included) Steak, soy sauce, sugar, cornstarch, bell peppers, sherry	275	13	42
Butterfly Prawns (each) (Deep-fried appetizers) Shrimp, cornstarch, egg whites, bacon, oil	62	3	37
Cantonese Barbecued Pork Pork, sherry, sugar, soy sauce, bean sauce, hoisin sauce, honey, oil, garlic, chickpeas	354	14	37
Cantonese Barbecued Spareribs Pork ribs, hoisin sauce, soy sauce, honey, sherry, oil	1255	78	56
Chicken Lo Mein Chicken, egg noodles, soy sauce, egg, celery, oil, onions, sherry	232	15	56

CHINESE	Calories per serving	Fat (Grams)	% Calories as fat
Chicken with Almonds (Rice not included) Chicken, mushrooms, bell pepper, pineapple, almonds, cornstarch, water chestnuts, bamboo shoots, sherry, sugar, oil, egg white, onions	256	13	47
Chicken with Orange Flavor (Rice not included) Chicken, egg whites, soy sauce, sherry, cornstarch, orange, oil, onions	611	31	45
Chicken with Peanuts (Rice not included) Chicken, peanuts, cornstarch, sugar, egg white, soy sauce, sherry, oil, chili peppers, onions	590	34	52

CHINESE	Calories per serving	Fat (Grams)	% Calories as fat
Chicken with Walnuts (Rice not included) Chicken, walnuts, sherry, egg white, soy sauce, cornstarch, oil, chili peppers, mushrooms, water chestnuts, bamboo shoots, bell pepper, onions, chickpeas	511	33	58
Chicken Wonton Soup Chicken, pork, sherry, cornstarch, soy sauce, egg white, broth, oil	215	8	32
Chinese Curried Chicken (Rice not included) Chicken, sherry, soy sauce, potatoes, onions, oil, garlic, sugar	259	13	46
Cold Spicy Noodles Egg noodles, bean sprouts, peanut butter, soy sauce, sugar, oil	304	15	44

CHINESE	Calories per serving	Fat (Grams)	% Calories as fat
Crispy Beef (Rice not included) Steak, eggs, soy sauce, cornstarch, sherry, oil	301	18	53
Drunken Chicken (Cold dish) Chicken, white wine, sugar	168	2	9
Egg Drop Soup Eggs, broth, cornstarch, oil, sugar, onions	119	7	51
Eggplant in Chili Garlic Sauce (Rice not included) Eggplant, sugar, sherry, soy sauce, bean sauce, oil, chili peppers, garlic	206	13	55
Fish Slices in Hot Vinegar Sauce (Rice not included) Fish, pork, sherry, cornstarch, chili peppers, mushrooms, sugar, soy sauce, broth, oil, egg, onions	369	19	47

CHINESE	Calories per serving	Fat (Grams)	% Calories as fat
Fried Dumplings (each) Pork, sherry, soy sauce, flour, oil, cabbage, onions	124	7	53
Fried Rice Rice, eggs, ham, shrimp, cornstarch, peas, soy sauce, oil, onions, mushrooms	320	13	37
Fried Wontons with Shrimp Filling (each) Shrimp, egg white, bamboo shoots, soy sauce, oil, onions, sherry	39	2	48
Ginger Beef (Rice not included) Steak, soy sauce, sherry, cornstarch, parsley, oil, sugar, onion	728	48	59
Hacked Chicken Chicken, peanuts, celery, peanut butter, soy sauce, sugar, oil, sherry	432	23	47

Chinese	Calories per serving	Fat (Grams)	% Calories as fat
Hot Chinese Cabbage Cabbage, soy sauce, sugar, oil, chili peppers	356	27	68
Hot and Sour Soup Chicken, broth, bean curd, bamboo shoots, mushrooms, soy sauce, egg, cornstarch, oil	101	4	33
Lamb with Scallions (Rice not included) Lamb, soy sauce, sherry, oil, scallions, sugar	477	34	63
Lemon Chicken (Rice not included) Chicken, egg, sherry, cornstarch, sugar, broth, soy sauce, bell pepper, oil, garlic, onions	576	33	51
Lobster Cantonese (Rice not included) Lobster, pork, black beans, cornstarch, soy sauce, sherry, broth, bell peppers, eggs, oil	168	10	55

CHINESE	Calories per serving	Fat (Grams)	% Calories as fat
Mandarin Pancakes (each) Flour, oil	60	2	32
Minced Beef with String Beans (Rice not included) Ground beef, green beans, water chestnuts, broth, soy sauce, cornstarch, oil, sugar	670	49	66
Mixed Vegetables (Rice not included) Snow peas, bamboo shoots, water chestnuts, corn, mushrooms, broth, cornstarch, oil, sugar	410	18	40
Moo Goo Gai Pan (Rice not included) Chicken, mushrooms, corn, sherry, broth, sugar, cornstarch, oil	254	8	29
Moo Shu Pork (Pancakes not included) Pork, eggs, mushrooms, sherry, soy sauce, cornstarch, cabbage, bamboo shoots, onions	387	26	61

CHINESE	Calories per serving	Fat (Grams)	% Calories as fat
Paper Chicken (each) Chicken, sherry, hoisin sauce, sugar, soy sauce, oil, mushrooms	124	7	51
Peking Duck (Pancakes not included) Duck, honey, sherry, onions	773	57	67
Peking Smoked Chicken (Cold dish) Chicken, sherry, sugar, soy sauce, oil	316	13	37
Peking Pure Shrimp (Rice not included) Shrimp, egg white, green onions, cornstarch, sherry, oil, sugar	379	27	65
Pineapple Chicken (Rice not included) Chicken, onions, celery, water chestnuts, pineapple, pineapple juice, soy sauce, cornstarch, oil	633	30	42
Plain Rice	111	0	0

CHINESE	Calories per serving	Fat (Grams)	% Calories as fat
Pork with Garlic Sauce (Rice not included) Pork, water chestnuts, soy sauce, cornstarch, sherry, bean sauce, sugar, oil, garlic, onions	967	67	63
Shrimp Cantonese (Rice not included) Shrimp, pork, bell pepper, black beans, soy sauce, cornstarch, egg white, oil	257	18	64
Shrimp Fu Yung Shrimp, eggs, peas, water chestnuts, onions, sherry, cornstarch, oil, soy sauce	251	20	70
Shrimp with Cashew Nuts (Rice not included) Shrimp, cashews, mushrooms, water chestnuts, sherry, soy sauce, oil, sugar	239	17	62

CHINESE	Calories per serving	Fat (Grams)	% Calories as fat
Shrimp with Green Peas	656	41	57
(Rice not included) Shrimp, egg, cornstarch, peas, ham, oil, onions, sherry			
Sizzling Rice Soup with Shrimp and Chicken	242	11	41
Chicken, rice, cornstarch, shrimp, egg whites, corn, peas, mushrooms, oil, sugar, egg white, sherry			
Smoked Chicken	316	13	37
(Cold dish) Chicken, sherry, sugar, oil			
Smoked Fish	192	9	43
(Deep-fried appetizer) Fish, sherry, soy sauce, sugar, onions			

CHINESE	Calories per serving	Fat (Grams)	% Calories as fat
Snow Peas, Water Chestnuts, and Bamboo Shoots (Rice not included) Snow peas, mushrooms, bamboo shoots, water chestnuts, soy sauce, sherry, oil, onions	131	8	54
Soy Sauce Chicken (Rice not included) Chicken, sherry, sugar, soy sauce, oil, onions	307	19	55
Spicy Shredded Beef (Rice not included) Steak, egg white, cornstarch, sherry, soy sauce, sugar, water chestnuts, broth, oil, onions	403	30	66

CHINESE	Calories per serving	Fat (Grams)	% Calories as fat
Spring Rolls with Shrimp and Chicken Filling (each) Shrimp, chicken, sherry, mushrooms, water chestnuts, bean sprouts, bamboo shoots, cornstarch, egg white, soy sauce, oil, garlic, spring roll dough	148	10	58
Steamed Dumplings with Pork and Shrimp (each) Pork, shrimp, mushrooms, sherry, soy sauce, sugar, wontons	44	2	47
Steamed Fish Fish, sherry, mushrooms, soy sauce, oil, onions	294	16	50
Subgum Soup Chicken, shrimp, broth, mushrooms, cabbage, cornstarch, oil	87	3	26

CHINESE	Calories per serving	Fat (Grams)	% Calories as fat
Sweet and Sour Fish (Rice not included) Fish, sherry, cornstarch, flour, onion, tomato, sugar, soy sauce, oil, garlic	486	25	45
Sweet and Sour Pork (Deep-fried pork, rice not included) Pork, cornstarch, sherry, egg, water chestnuts, bamboo shoots, bell pepper, pineapple, pineapple juice, soy sauce, oil	596	32	48
Szechwan Spiced Shrimp (Rice not included) Shrimp, sherry, soy sauce, flour, cornstarch, egg, sugar, catsup, oil, chili peppers	414	22	48
Twice Cooked Pork (Rice not included) Pork, bell pepper, cabbage, bean sauce, soy sauce, sherry, oil, onions, sugar	958	77	72

CHINESE	Calories per serving	Fat (Grams)	% Calories as fat
Velvet Chicken Lo Mein	354	12	31
Chicken, noodles, egg white, cornstarch, bean sprouts, mushrooms, broth, oil, soy sauce			
Velvet Corn Soup with Crabmeat	60	1	18
Crabmeat, egg whites, milk, broth, cornstarch			
Wonton Soup with Shrimp and Pork	228	13	51
Pork, shrimp, egg, broth, sugar, sherry, soy sauce, oil, watercress, wontons			

MEXICAN FOOD

The best rule of thumb when you're eating Mexican food is to keep it simple. The basics of Mexican cuisine, such as tortillas, beans, and corn, are low in fat. Adding on layers of cheese and sour cream is what turns Mexican food into calorie- and fat-laden dishes to be avoided. Stick with chicken tacos, burritos, and enchiladas rather than the beef variety. They are generally lower in fat. When eating out, ask that the cheese and sour cream be left off or served on the side. You may, however, allow yourself generous portions of lettuce, tomato, and salsa toppings. Choose soft tacos and burritos over the fried variety and you'll save on fat there, too. If you're concerned about saturated fat and cholesterol, be forewarned that traditional Mexican recipes call for lard, which is high in both. More trendy Mexican restaurants tend to use vegetable oils instead.

If you're preparing Mexican food at home, substitute vegetable oil for lard and reduce the amount the recipe calls for. You can also try using lower-fat cheeses and sour cream. But don't overdo. Even these lower-calorie substitutes can add extra pounds if not used judiciously.

MEXICAN BEST BETS

Black Beans • Cantaloupe Soup •
Capirotada • Flour Tortilla • Shrimp
Enchilada • Soft Chicken Taco •
Tortilla Soup

MEXICAN	Calories per serving	Fat (Grams)	% Calories as fat
Almond Sponge Cake Almonds, eggs, sugar, flour, brandy	224	12	49
Avocado Soup (*Crema de Aguacate*) Avocados, half-and-half, chicken broth, sherry, sour cream	215	18	77
Beef Burrito Tortilla, beef, garlic, onion, tomatoes, lard	456	18	35
Beef Chimichanga Tortilla, beef, oil, tomatoes, pinto beans, onion, lard	740	51	63
Beef Enchilada Beef, chili sauce, tomato sauce, cheese, olives, tortillas, lard, tomatoes, onions	572	33	52
Beef Taco Beef, chili sauce, tomato sauce, cheese, onion, tortillas, garlic, tomatoes, lard	541	29	48

MEXICAN	Calories per serving	Fat (Grams)	% Calories as fat
Black Beans (*Frijoles Negros*) Black beans, lard, sour cream	324	8	23
Cantaloupe Soup (*Sopa de Melon Escribe*) Half-and-half, potato, cantaloupe, sherry	90	3	25
Capirotada (Dessert) French bread, cheese, prunes, dates, banana, almonds, sugar, eggs, flour, whipped cream	497	14	26
Cheese Enchilada Tortilla, cheese, olives, onions	265	18	61
Chicken Breast with Chilis Chicken breast, peanut oil, green chilies, milk, sour cream, cheese, butter	614	42	63

Mexican	Calories per serving	Fat (Grams)	% Calories as fat
Chicken Burrito with Sour Cream Chicken, onions, garlic, oil, tomatoes, flour, sour cream, tortilla	330	13	35
Chicken Chilaquiles Fried corn tortilla, chicken, tomatoes, cheese, sour cream, bacon fat	406	25	56
Chicken Enchilada Fried corn tortilla, chicken, cheese, tomatoes, sour cream, chili peppers	197	11	52
Chicken Taco with Sour Cream Fried corn tortilla, chicken, tomatoes, sour cream, garlic, tomato sauce, chicken broth	119	7	51
Chili with Meat (*Chili con Carne*) Beef, flour, broth, lard	927	74	72

MEXICAN	Calories per serving	Fat (Grams)	% Calories as fat
Chili with Meat and Beans (*Chile con Carne y Frijoles*) Beef, pinto beans, beef broth, tomatoes, lard, onions	883	60	63
Chilies with Cheese Green chilies, tomatoes, onions, milk, cheese	374	29	69
Chilies Rellenos (Stuffed Chilies) Chilies, oil, cheese, egg	237	19	71
Crabmeat Enchilada Fried corn tortilla, crabmeat, butter, cheese, whipping cream, chili peppers	325	23	64
Crabmeat Nachos Tortilla chips, cheese, avocado, butter, crabmeat, tomato, chili pepper, sherry	131	11	74

MEXICAN	Calories per serving	Fat (Grams)	% Calories as fat
Enchilada El Mole Fried corn tortillas, pork, cheese, chicken broth, lard, plantain, tomatoes, chili peppers	379	24	57
Enchiladas Rancheras Chilies, fried corn tortillas, cheese, chicken, sour cream, avocados, chili peppers, broth, cornstarch	459	31	61
Fish in Green Sauce Fish, green chilies, tomatoes, olive oil, lime juice	448	20	40
Flan Milk, sugar, eggs	278	13	44
Flour Tortilla Flour, shortening	168	4	23
Green Bean and Zucchini Squash Salad Green beans, zucchini, peaches, avocado	146	11	67

Mexican	Calories per serving	Fat (Grams)	% Calories as fat
Green Chicken Enchilada Fried corn tortilla, chicken, chicken broth, tomatoes, sour cream, cheese, chili peppers	405	22	50
Green Chili Sauce ($^1/_2$ cup) Chicken broth, green chilies, onions, butter, tomatoes, sugar	100	5	44
Guacamole Avocados, tomatoes, onions, chili peppers	178	16	80
Huevos Rancheros Corn tortilla, eggs, oil, salsa	724	53	67
Margarita Tequila, triple sec, lemon juice	220	< 1	0
Mexican Rice White rice, oil, tomatoes, chicken broth, peas, carrots	157	7	37

MEXICAN	Calories per serving	Fat (Grams)	% Calories as fat
Nachos Tortilla chips, cheese, refried beans, ground beef, sour cream, guacamole	168	12	60
Onion and Cheese Quesadillas Tortillas, onions, butter, cheese, sour cream, tomatoes, lettuce	343	19	51
Plantains (*Platanos Dulces*) [Sweet Bananas] Plantain, butter, sugar, wine, whipped cream	299	13	40
Pumpkin Blossom Soup Pumpkin flowers, butter, onions, broth	73	5	58
Red Sauce (1/2 cup) Tomatoes, chilies, onions, lime juice	68	1	8

MEXICAN	Calories per serving	Fat (Grams)	% Calories as fat
Red Snapper Veracruz Red snapper, olive oil, green olives, onion, tomatoes, lime juice, chili peppers	403	20	46
Refried Beans Pinto beans, lard, cheese, tortilla chips, onions	285	15	49
Sangria (Wine Cooler) Wine, club soda, brandy, peaches, lemons, oranges	164	tr	0
Sangrita Tomato juice, oranges, limes, sugar, chili peppers	87	<1	3
Shrimp Enchilada Fried corn tortilla, shrimp, tomatoes, tomato sauce, butter	231	9	35
Soft Chicken Taco Fried corn tortilla, tomatoes, chicken, chicken broth	229	8	31

MEXICAN	Calories per serving	Fat (Grams)	% Calories as fat
Sweet Tamales (*Tamales de Dulce*) Masa harina flour, sugar, margarine, lard, chicken broth, almonds, raisins	273	14	47
Tamales Chicken, chicken broth, lard, tamale dough	241	19	71
Tortilla Soup (*Sopa de Tortilla*) Tortillas, chicken broth, cheddar cheese	143	6	35
Tostada with Guacamole Fried corn tortilla, cheese, guacamole	53	4	61
Tequila Sunrise Tequila, orange juice, grenadine	189	<1	1
White Rice with Corn White rice, oil, chicken broth, corn	327	13	37

ITALIAN FOOD

Italian dishes live up to their reputation for being rich and filling. Pasta, whether it's smothered, stuffed, or steamed, is a mainstay in Italian cooking. But unadulterated pasta has an undeserved reputation for being "fattening." It's the company pasta generally keeps, like cream sauces and cheese, that make it high-calorie. One-half cup of plain pasta provides only about 100 calories and less than one gram of fat. As in Greek cuisine, one ingredient you should watch out for is olive oil. Though olive oil is low in saturated fat and high in monounsaturated fats (good for your arteries), it contains the same number of calories per tablespoon (120) as any other fat and should therefore be kept to a minimum. Ask the waiter if the oil can be served on the side or at least cut by half when your dish is being prepared. And skip the antipasti; it is generally doused in olive oil. Cheese is another ubiquitous ingredient in Italian food that you should try to minimize. An alternative to cheese-laden dishes: a low-fat pasta dish such as Thin Spaghetti with Red Clam Sauce, topped with a tablespoon of Parmesan cheese.

ITALIAN BEST BETS

Chick-peas and Pasta Soup • Fresh Fruit Whip • Potato Gnocchi with Pesto Sauce • Rice Cake • Stewed Squid with Tomatoes and Peas • Sweetbreads Braised with Tomatoes and Peas • Thin Spaghetti with Eggplant • Thin Spaghetti with Red Clam Sauce

ITALIAN	Calories per serving	Fat (Grams)	% Calories as fat
Anchovies (*Acciughe*, Antipasti) Anchovies, olive oil	141	11	68
Asparagus Salad (*Insalata de Asparagi*) Asparagus, olive oil	188	15	72
Baked Oysters with Oil and Parsley (*Ostriche alla Moda di Taranto*) Oysters, bread crumbs, olive oil	147	11	66
Baked Oysters with Parmesan Cheese (*Ostriche alla Parmigiana*) Oysters, Parmesan cheese, bread crumbs, butter	135	8	55
Beef Braised in Red Wine Sauce (*Stracotto al Barolo*) Roast, butter, onion, carrot, celery, red wine, broth, tomatoes	895	54	55

ITALIAN	Calories per serving	Fat (Grams)	% Calories as fat
Black-eyed Peas and Sausages with Tomato Sauce (*Fagioli dall'Occhio con Salsicce*) Black-eyed peas, sausage, onion, olive oil, carrot, celery, tomatoes	654	50	68
Broiled Mussels and Clams on the Half Shell (*Cozze e Vongole Passate ai Ferri*) Clams, mussels, parsley, olive oil, bread crumbs, tomatoes	249	16	58
Cappelletti in Broth (*Cappelletti in Brodo*) Cappelletti, broth	305	13	40
Cappelletti with Butter and Heavy Cream (*Cappelletti con la Panna*) Cappelletti, cream, olive oil, butter, Parmesan cheese	634	40	56

ITALIAN	Calories per serving	Fat (Grams)	% Calories as fat
Cappelletti Filled with Meat and Cheese (*Cappelletti*) Pork, butter, chicken, mortadella, ricotta cheese, egg yolk, Parmesan cheese, pasta dough	296	13	40
Caramelized Almond Candy (*Croccante*) Almonds, sugar	353	18	46
Chick-Peas and Pasta Soup (*Zuppa di Ceci e Maltagliati*) Chick-peas, olive oil, tomatoes, broth, macaroni, Parmesan cheese	269	11	37
Coffee Ice with Whipped Cream (*Granita de Caffe con Panna*) Espresso coffee, sugar, cream	135	13	84

ITALIAN	Calories per serving	Fat (Grams)	% Calories as fat
Cold Salmon Foam (*Spuma Fredda di Salmone*) Salmon, olive oil, whipping cream	355	32	80
Escarole and Rice Soup (*Zuppa di Scarola e Riso*) Escarole, broth, rice, Parmesan cheese, butter	235	13	51
Espresso Coffee Ice Cream with Hot Chocolate Sauce Espresso coffee, egg yolks, sugar, cream, cocoa	403	30	68
Fettuccine with White Clam Sauce (*Fettuccine al Sugo di Vongole Bianco*) Fettucine, clams, green onions, olive oil, white wine, butter, Parmesan cheese	490	34	62

ITALIAN	Calories per serving	Fat (Grams)	% Calories as fat
Fettucini Tossed in Cream and Butter (*Fettucini al l'Alfredo*) Fettucini, butter, cream, egg, flour, Parmesan cheese	425	27	56
Fillet of Sole with Piquant Tomato Sauce (*Filetti di Sogliola con Pomodoro e Capperi*) Sole, onion, olive oil, tomatoes, capers	423	24	50
Fresh Fruit Whip (*Frullati di Frutta*) Milk, sugar, fruit, liqueur	164	3	16
Glazed Bread Pudding (*Budino di Pane Caramellato*) Bread, sugar, butter, milk, raisins, flour, eggs, pine nuts, rum	299	15	44
Green Bean Salad (*Fagiolini Verdi in Insalata*) Green beans, olive oil	88	7	71

ITALIAN	Calories per serving	Fat (Grams)	% Calories as fat
Lentil Soup (*Zuppa di Lenticchie*) Lentils, carrots, celery, tomatoes, Parmesan cheese, prosciutto, butter, olive oil, broth	400	21	47
Meat-Stuffed Pasta Rolls (*Cannelloni*) Flour, milk, butter, onions, olive oil, ground beef, egg, Parmesan cheese, ricotta cheese, tomatoes	814	57	63
Open-Faced Italian Omelet with Artichokes (*Frittata di Carciofi*) Eggs, artichokes, olive oil, Parmesan cheese, butter	283	24	76
Open-Faced Italian Omelet with Asparagus (*Frittata di Asparagi*) Eggs, asparagus, Parmesan cheese, butter	296	21	64

ITALIAN	Calories per serving	Fat (Grams)	% Calories as fat
Open-Faced Italian Omelet with Cheese (*Frittata al Formaggio*) Eggs, Parmesan cheese, butter	308	24	71
Open-Faced Italian Omelet with Green Beans (*Frittata con Fagiolini Verdi*) Eggs, green beans, Parmesan cheese, butter	301	23	69
Open-Faced Italian Omelet with Tomatoes, Onions, and Basil (*Frittata al Pomodoro e Basilico*) Eggs, tomatoes, olive oil, Parmesan cheese, butter, basil	408	35	77
Pan-Broiled Steak with Marsala and Hot Pepper Sauce (*Bistecca alla Diavola*) Beef steak, olive oil, white wine, red wine, tomato paste	913	50	49

ITALIAN	Calories per serving	Fat (Grams)	% Calories as fat
Pan-Roasted Chicken with Garlic, Rosemary, and White Wine (*Pollo Arrosto in Tegame*) Chicken, butter, oil, white wine	547	36	59
Peppers and Anchovies (*Peperoni e Acciughe, Antipasti* Bell peppers, anchovies, garlic, olive oil	64	5	73
Potato Gnocchi with Pesto Sauce (*Gnocchi di Patate con Pesto*) Potato, flour, Parmesan cheese, pine nuts, romano cheese, butter	391	15	34

ITALIAN	Calories per serving	Fat (Grams)	% Calories as fat
Red Snapper with Sauteed Mushrooms (*Pagello con i Funghi Trifolati*) Snapper, olive oil, mushrooms, butter, onion, carrot, anchovy, parsley, white wine, broth	480	26	48
Rice Cake (*Torta di Riso*) Milk, sugar, rice, eggs, almonds, butter, rum, bread crumbs	375	13	31
Risotto with Meat Sauce (*Risotto col Ragu*) Broth, chuck, oil, onions, rice, Parmesan cheese, butter, celery, carrot, white wine, milk, tomatoes	369	7	16

ITALIAN	Calories per serving	Fat (Grams)	% Calories as fat
Risotto with Parmesan Cheese (*Risotto alla Parmigiana*) Rice, broth, onions, butter, oil, Parmesan cheese	443	19	38
Risotto with Zucchini (*Risotto con le Zucchine*) Rice, zucchini, onions, oil, broth, butter, Parmesan cheese	507	27	48
Rolled Stuffed Breast of Veal (*Petto di Vitello Arrotolato*) Veal, pancetta, butter, oil, white wine	576	36	56
Rum-and-Coffee-Flavored Chocolate Layer Cake (*Il Diplomatico*) Eggs, sugar, rum, espresso coffee, pound cake, semisweet chocolate, butter, whipped cream	565	42	67

ITALIAN	Calories per serving	Fat (Grams)	% Calories as fat
Sauteed Chicken Breast Fillets with Lemon and Parsley (*Petti di Pollo alla Senese*) Chicken, oil, butter, parsley, lemon	356	23	59
Sauteed Chicken Livers with Sage (*Fegatini di Pollo alla Salvia*) Chicken livers, onion, butter, white wine	255	14	49
Sauteed Green Beans with Butter and Cheese (*Fagiolini Verdi al Burro e Formaggio*) Green beans, butter, Parmesan cheese	104	9	78
Sauteed Peas with Prosciutto Florentine Style (*Pisellini alla Fiorentina*) Peas, prosciutto, olive oil, parsley	155	11	61

Italian	Calories per serving	Fat (Grams)	% Calories as fat
Sauteed Veal Chops with Sage and White Wine (*Nodini di Vitello alla Salvia*) Veal chops, oil, flour, butter, white wine, sage	418	26	55
Sauteed Veal Scaloppine with Lemon Sauce (*Scaloppine di Vitello al Limone*) Veal, oil, butter, flour, lemon	488	30	56
Sauteed Veal Scaloppine with Marsala (*Scaloppine di Vitello al Marsala*) Veal, oil, flour, wine, butter	513	31	54
Shrimp and Vegetable Salad (*Insalata Russa con Gamberi*) Shrimp, green beans, potatoes, carrots, peas, beets, olive oil, mayonnaise	869	81	84

ITALIAN	Calories per serving	Fat (Grams)	% Calories as fat
Shrimps with Oil and Lemon (*Gamberetti all 'Olio e Limone Antipasti*) Shrimp, celery, carrot, olive oil, lemon juice	203	19	82
Spaghetti with Garlic and Oil (*Spaghetti "Ajo e Ojo"*) Spaghetti, olive oil, garlic	688	32	42
Spinach and Ricotta Gnocchi (*Gnocchi Verdi*) Spinach, onions, butter, ham, ricotta cheese, flour, egg, Parmesan cheese	367	21	52
Stewed Squid with Tomatoes and Peas (*Calamari e Piselli alla Livornese*) Squid, onions, tomatoes, parsley, peas	210	3	13

Italian	Calories per serving	Fat (Grams)	% Calories as fat
Stuffed Breaded Veal Chops (*Costolette alla Milanese*) Veal chops, eggs, bread crumbs, butter	454	29	56
Sweetbreads Braised with Tomatoes and Peas (*Animelle con Pomodori e Piselli*) Sweetbreads, carrot, celery, green onions, butter, oil, tomatoes, peas	395	16	37
Thin Pan-Broiled Steaks with Tomatoes and Olives (*Fettine di Manzo alla Sorrentina*) Beef steaks, onion, olive oil, tomatoes, olives	372	24	59
Thin Spaghetti with Eggplant (*Spaghettini con le Melanzane*) Eggplant, olive oil, spaghetti, tomatoes	558	12	19

ITALIAN	Calories per serving	Fat (Grams)	% Calories as fat
Thin Spaghetti with Red Clam Sauce (*Spaghettini alle Vongole*) Clams, spaghetti, tomatoes, olive oil	564	12	20
Tomatoes Stuffed with Shrimp (*Pomodori Ripieni di Tonno, Antipasti*) Tomatoes, shrimp, egg, olive oil, mustard	249	20	72
Tomatoes Stuffed with Tuna and Capers (*Pomodori Ripieni di Tonno, Antipasti*) Tomatoes, tuna, mayonnaise, mustard, capers, egg	324	25	69

ITALIAN	Calories per serving	Fat (Grams)	% Calories as fat
Tortellini Filled with Parsley and Ricotta with Tomato and Cream Sauce (*Tortellini di Prezzemolo di Sugo di Pomodoro e Panna*) Flour, milk, butter, egg, parsley, ricotta cheese, Parmesan cheese, onions, carrots, celery, tomatoes, cream	594	38	58
Veal Stew with Sage and White Wine (*Spezzalmo di Vitello alla Salvia*) Veal, green onions, oil, butter, flour, sage, white wine	594	32	48
Veal Stew with Tomatoes and Peas (*Spezzalmo di Vitello coi Piselli*) Veal, green onions, oil, butter, peas, tomatoes	579	35	55

ITALIAN	Calories per serving	Fat (Grams)	% Calories as fat
Vegetable Soup (*Minestrone di Romagna*) Zucchini, onion, carrots, potato, white beans, green beans,cabbage, butter, olive oil, tomatoes, broth, Parmesan cheese, celery	309	23	66
Zucchini Stuffed with Meat and Cheese (*Zucchine con Ripieno di Carne e Formaggio*) Zucchini, onion, oil, parsley, tomato paste, milk, bread, beef, egg, prosciutto	270	15	51

FRENCH FOOD

The French are known for their food. Anyone who has been to Paris will tell you it's hard to find a bad meal. But if you're counting calories, French cuisine is off limits—or at least limited to very special occasions. The reason is simple: The key ingredient in French cooking is butter, butter, and more butter, laced with a touch of cream for extra richness. You can't escape it by ordering vegetable dishes because they, too, are loaded with the key ingredient.

If you do find yourself in a French restaurant, fill up on fresh *Baguettes (sans* the butter). The bread is low-fat, so use it to curb your appetite before the more fat-laden main dish arrives. Unlike other cuisines, where soups are a good choice, most French soups are cream-based and therefore loaded with fat and calories. Be sure to find out if fat is lurking in seemingly low-cal dishes. For example, Chicken Poached in Wine, Herbs, and Vegetables sounds like a good choice, but because the skin is left on (and included in the calorie count) and butter is added, 57 percent of its calories come from fat. That's less than the 70 percent or more of calories found in several other French dishes, but it is still too much fat for someone watching their fat and calorie intake.

About half of the dishes listed below provide 30 percent or less calories from fat. For the rest, however, the term "best bets" is used rather loosely, indicating dishes that contain less than 50 percent of calories as fat—about as low as you'll find in most French dishes.

FRENCH BEST BETS

Apples Baked with Rum, Raisins, and Cream • Apricot Sherbet • Baguette • Egg Bread • Mold of Parslied Ham in Aspic • Plums Baked in Custard • Puree of Rice and Turnips • Scallop Bouillabaisse • Spice Cake • Spinach Braised with Onions • Veal Stew with Carrots, Onions, Potatoes, and Peas

FRENCH	Calories per serving	Fat (Grams)	% Calories as fat
Apples Baked with Rum, Raisins, and Cream (*Gratin de Pommes, Normandie—Clafouti aux Pommes*) Apples, currants, butter, sugar, rum, flour, cream, eggs	316	10	28
Apricot Sherbet (*Mousse a l'Abricot, Glacée*) Apricots, egg white, sugar	172	tr	0
Baguette [¼ *baguette*] Flour, yeast	124	< 1	2
Beef Stew with Herbs, Cheese, and Garlic (*Boeuf au Pistou*) Beef, broth, onion, garlic, tomatoes, wine, flour, butter, salt pork, olive oil, Parmesan cheese, tomato paste	591	42	64

FRENCH	Calories per serving	Fat (Grams)	% Calories as fat
Beef Stew with Onions and Red Wine (*Boeuf aux Oignons*) Beef, broth, onion, garlic, tomatoes, wine, flour, butter, salt pork, olive oil	566	41	66
Beef Tongue with Curry (*Langue de Boeuf Braisee, Calcutta*) Tongue, onions, butter, flour, broth, white wine, garlic, currants, apple, cream	786	56	64
Beef Tongue with Sweet and Sour Sauce, Onions, and Raisins (*Langue de Boeuf, a l'Aigre-Douce*) Tongue, onions, carrots, celery, ham, butter, broth, currants, mustard, wine	705	50	64

FRENCH	Calories per serving	Fat (Grams)	% Calories as fat
Braised Pot Roast with Wine, Tomatoes, and Provencal Flavorings (*Boeuf en Daube a la Provencale*) Beef, lard, red wine, olive oil, garlic, onions, carrots, tomatoes, ham	368	22	55
Braised Stuffed Shoulder of Lamb (*Epaule d'Agneau Farcie, Viroflay*) Lamb, butter, mushrooms, oil, spinach, green onions, garlic, broth, bread crumbs, pork fat, egg, carrot, white wine, cornstarch	654	44	61
Brioche Flour, eggs, yeast, sugar, butter	226	16	63

FRENCH	Calories per serving	Fat (Grams)	% Calories as fat
Broccoli Gratineed with Cheese Sauce (*Gratin de Brocoli, Mornay*) Broccoli, butter, flour, milk, Parmesan cheese	315	25	71
Broccoli Simmered in Cream (*Brocoli Etuves a la Creme*) Broccoli, cream, cornstarch	273	25	82
Broccoli with Bread Crumbs and Eggs (*Brocoli Sautes a la Polonaise*) Broccoli, butter, bread crumbs, egg	263	21	70
Broiled Eggplant Slices (*Aubergines en Tranches, Gratinees*) Eggplant, olive oil, garlic, tomatoes, bread crumbs	525	38	65

FRENCH	Calories per serving	Fat (Grams)	% Calories as fat
Casserole Chicken with Wine (*Poularde Pochee a l'Estragon*) Chicken, carrots, onions, butter, white wine, broth, flour, cream	848	68	72
Catalonian Pepper and Leek Soup (*Soupe Catalane aux Poivrons*) Ham, onions, bell peppers, garlic, flour, broth, rice, egg yolks, olive oil, leeks	301	20	60
Celery Soup with Potatoes, Leeks, and Rice (*Potage Celestine*) Leeks, celery, broth, rice, butter, potatoes, milk	352	19	49

FRENCH	Calories per serving	Fat (Grams)	% Calories as fat
Chicken Bouillabaisse (*Bouillabaisse de Poulet*) Chicken, onions, olive oil, tomato, garlic, white wine, chicken broth	641	41	57
Chicken in a Cold Dish (*Chaud-froid de Poulet, Morvandelle*) Chicken, cream, egg yolk, wine, carrot, onion, celery, butter, broth	855	66	69
Chicken Poached in Wine, Herbs, and Vegetables (*Poulet Poche au Vin Blanc*) Chicken, carrots, onions, celery, white wine, broth, butter	556	35	57

FRENCH	Calories per serving	Fat (Grams)	% Calories as fat
Chocolate Burnt Almond Ice Cream (*Glace au Chocolat, Pralinee*) Almonds, sugar, chocolate, cream	712	59	74
Chocolate Cake (*Le Glorieux*) Chocolate, cornstarch, liqueur, eggs, sugar, butter	332	18	48
Cream of Cauliflower and Watercress Soup (*Potage de la Fontaine Dureau*) Cauliflower, watercress, butter, leeks, flour, cream	285	25	79
Cream of Cucumber Soup (*Potage aux Concombres*) Cucumber, onions, butter, broth, sour cream	260	18	63

FRENCH	Calories per serving	Fat (Grams)	% Calories as fat
Cream of Fresh Asparagus Soup (*Potage Creme D'Asperges Vertes*) Asparagus, onions, butter, flour, milk, cream, egg yolk	378	32	77
Cream of Mushroom Soup (*Potage aux Champignons, Ile de France*) Mushrooms, onions, butter, flour, milk, cream	387	32	74
Cream of Onion Soup (*Potage creme aux Oignons, Soubise*) Onions, butter, flour, broth, white wine, rice, milk, cream	414	30	65
Cream of Spinach Soup (*Potage a la Florentine*) Spinach, onions, butter, broth, rice, cream, egg yolks	330	24	67

FRENCH	Calories per serving	Fat (Grams)	% Calories as fat
Croissant Flour, egg, oil, milk, butter, yeast, sugar	197	14	64
Egg Bread (*Pain Brioche*) Flour, yeast, sugar, milk, eggs, butter	122	5	40
Eggplant Baked with Cheese and Tomatoes (*Gratin d'Aubergines, Provencal*) Eggplant, onions, tomatoes, olive oil, garlic, cheese	258	17	60
Eggplant with Bechamel (*Aubergines en Persillade, Gratinees*) Eggplant, flour, butter, milk, bread crumbs, garlic, tomatoes, olive oil	600	45	67

FRENCH	Calories per serving	Fat (Grams)	% Calories as fat
Eggplant Souffle (*Souffle d'Aubergines en Persillade*) Eggplant, olive oil, garlic, tomatoes, bread crumbs, flour, milk, butter, Parmesan cheese, eggs, onions	815	60	67
Fish Stew with Mayonnaise (*Bourride*) Fish, onion, carrots, leeks, olive oil, tomatoes, white wine, bread crumbs, garlic, egg yolks, clam juice	902	67	67
Gratin of Potatoes and Endive (*Gratin Dauphinois aux Endives*) Potatoes, butter, onions, cheese, endive	229	18	69
Liver Pate (*Terrine de Foie de Porc*) Pork fat, liver, rice, eggs, cognac, broth	280	27	87

FRENCH	Calories per serving	Fat (Grams)	% Calories as fat
Meringue Nut Cake with Butter Cream Frosting and Filling (*Le Progres, La Dacquoise*) Flour, butter, almonds, sugar, cornstarch, eggs, milk, rum, chocolate	911	65	64
Mold of Parslied Ham in Aspic (*Jambon Persille*) Ham, vermouth, broth, garlic, onion, carrot, celery, egg white	234	6	23
Pate Baked in Brioche (*Pate de Foie et de Porc en Brioche*) Pork fat, pork, onions, garlic, bread crumbs, liver, cream, egg, cognac, brioche dough	433	31	65
Pea-Pod Soup (*Soupe Belle Potagere*) Peas, butter, leeks, flour, potatoes, onions, lettuce, milk, cream	327	20	55

FRENCH	Calories per serving	Fat (Grams)	% Calories as fat
Peppers in Garlic and Oil (*Salade de Poivrons, Provencale*) Bell peppers, garlic, oil	178	18	93
Plums Baked in Custard (*Flan aux Prunes— Clafouti aux Prunes*) Plums, sugar, eggs, flour, cream	305	10	28
Poached Chicken with Cheese Sauce (*Poulet Mornay, Gratine*) Chicken, flour, cheese, butter, carrots, celery, wine, onions, broth	785	55	63
Potatoes in Cream and Basil (*Pommes de Terre au Basilic*) Potatoes, flour, milk, cream, garlic, butter	327	21	57

FRENCH	Calories per serving	Fat (Grams)	% Calories as fat
Potato Pie with Herbs and Cream (*Tourte Limousine*) Potatoes, butter, sugar, onions, egg, cream, flour	336	28	74
Pound Cake (*Le Quatre Quarts*) Flour, butter, eggs, sugar, cornstarch	381	24	56
Puree of Rice and Turnips (*Gratin de Potiron d'Arpajon*) Rice, turnips, butter, milk	305	14	40
Puree of Rutabaga (*La Puree, Chateaux en Suede*) Rutabagas, butter, goose fat, flour, cream	277	22	70
Rice and Garlic Stuffing (*La Farce a l'Ail de Mme. Cassiot*) Rice, lard, garlic, mustard	409	39	86

FRENCH	Calories per serving	Fat (Grams)	% Calories as fat
Scallop Bouillabaisse (*Les Saint-Jacques en Bouillabaisse*) Scallops, onions, olive oil, tomatoes, white wine, clam juice	318	15	42
Spice Cake (*Pain d'Epices*) Honey, sugar, flour, almonds, citron, rum	475	5	10
Spinach Braised with Onions (*Gratin d'Epinards aux Oignons*) Spinach, onions, olive oil, flour, milk, cream	155	7	39
Stuffed Beef Roll (*La Paupiette de Gargantua*) Beef, mustard, onions, pork, fat, greens, egg, garlic, bread crumbs, ham, sausage, carrot, wine, broth, bacon, butter, collards, oil	797	67	76

FRENCH	Calories per serving	Fat (Grams)	% Calories as fat
Stuffed Lamb in Pastry (*Gigot Farci, en Croute*) Lamb, mushrooms, butter, onions, pate, egg, cognac, kidney, brioche dough	758	36	43
Stuffed Onions (*Oignons Farcis au Riz*) Onions, butter, rice, Parmesan cheese, cream, bread crumbs, white wine, broth	331	19	52
Stuffed Pumpkin (*Le Potiron Tout Rond*) Pumpkin, bread crumbs, butter, onions, cream, Swiss cheese	492	39	71
Sweet and Sour Onions Braised with Raisins (*Petits Oignons Aigre-doux*) Onions, broth, olive oil, sugar, tomato, currants, garlic	66	4	53

FRENCH	Calories per serving	Fat (Grams)	% Calories as fat
Swiss Chard with Cheese Sauce (*Blettes Gratinees*) Swiss chard, flour, egg yolk, cream, Parmesan cheese, butter	89	7	66
Tripe with Onions, Tomatoes, Wine, and Provencal Seasonings (*Tripes a la Nicoise*) Tripe, olive oil, pork, salt, tomatoes, garlic, white wine, broth, onions	585	38	59
Veal Stew with Carrots, Onions, Potatoes, and Peas (*Ragout de Veau, Printanier*) Veal, flour, oil, butter, onions, carrots, potatoes, wine, broth, tomatoes, mushrooms, cream, peas	638	32	46

FRENCH	Calories per serving	Fat (Grams)	% Calories as fat
Zucchini and Spinach Saute (*Courgettes aux Epinards*) Zucchini, spinach, olive oil, garlic, butter	151	11	64
Zucchini Sauteed in Butter (*Courgettes Sautees, Maitre d'Hotel*) Zucchini, butter, olive oil	119	11	83

JEWISH FOOD

Jewish cooking is in itself an international cuisine, based on the cooking of Jews who live all over the world. The variety of foods that can claim to be Jewish range from the Americanized Bagel to the traditional Kreplach. Because of Jewish dietary laws, you won't find meat dishes smothered in cheese or swimming in sour cream. And butter is rarely used. Instead, vegetable margarine or chicken fat is substituted. You will find Eastern European and Middle Eastern influences in a large number of dishes, which translates into meats and vegetables cooked in spicy broths for long periods of time to develop a rich flavor. More than one-half of the Jewish dishes listed in this section provide more than 50 percent of their calories from fat. The ones listed below provide 30 percent of calories from fat, or less.

JEWISH BEST BETS

Bagel • Beetroot Borscht • Cold Fish in Egg Sauce • Honeyed Sprouts • Iraqi Dried Fruit and Nut Salad • Kreplach • Krupnik • Persian Cucumber Salad • Prickly Pear Compote

JEWISH	Calories per serving	Fat (Grams)	% Calories as fat
Avocado with Smoked Salmon Avocado, smoked salmon, carrots	272	16	54
Bagel Flour, sugar, yeast, eggs	138	1	8
Bagels with Lox Bagels, butter, cream cheese, smoked salmon	457	27	52
Beef, Avocado, and Olive Salad (Moroccan Etalya) Beef, wine, bread, almonds, olives, pine nuts, onions, cucumbers, bell pepper, avocado	842	81	86
Beef Casserole with Dumplings Beef, beef fat, onions, flour, broth, tomatoes	886	71	72
Beef Stroganoff Beef, onions, margarine, mushrooms, flour, tomato puree, mustard, broth	563	41	65

Jewish	Calories per serving	Fat (Grams)	% Calories as fat
Beef Strudel Beef, margarine, chicken liver, flour, egg	734	36	44
Beef with Quinces Beef, beef fat, onions, quinces	202	11	47
Beetroot Borscht Beets, broth, carrot, sugar, eggs	140	3	19
Blini with Smoked Salmon Yeast, milk, flour, eggs, sugar, butter, smoked salmon, sour cream	377	17	40
Blintzes Flour, eggs, sugar, sour cream, cottage cheese, milk, butter, oil	418	31	68
Boulaf [On skewers] Lamb liver, oil	213	11	46
Cabbage Pirogi Cabbage, butter, flour, eggs, onions, margarine	397	26	59

JEWISH	Calories per serving	Fat (Grams)	% Calories as fat
Carrot and Chicken Tzimmes Chicken, chicken fat, potatoes, carrots, onions, sugar, flour	626	35	50
Carrots in Yogurt Carrots, egg, bread crumbs, oil, yogurt	255	16	55
Cheese Cake Flour, butter, sugar, eggs, cottage cheese, sour cream, cornstarch, raisins	442	28	56
Chicken Soup Chicken, onions, celery, parsnip, carrots, noodles	504	26	46
Chicken Stuffed with Almonds, Semolina, and Raisins Chicken, almonds, semolina, raisins, margarine, onions	1067	73	61

JEWISH	Calories per serving	Fat (Grams)	% Calories as fat
Cholent Brisket, lima beans, chicken fat, onions, potatoes	1184	69	53
Chopped Liver Chicken livers, onion, chicken fat, eggs, sugar	167	9	49
Cold Fish in Egg Sauce Cod, wine, eggs, butter	265	7	25
Date Cakes Flour, butter, dates	117	5	40
Dried Fruit Tzimmes Dried fruit, brisket, onion, potatoes, chicken fat, flour, sugar, wine	789	55	62
Eggplant and Cheese Souffle Eggplant, butter, cheese, cream cheese, eggs	444	34	70
Eggplant Salad (*Salat Chatzilim*) Eggplant, onions, oil, pepper, tomato, olives	145	7	40

Jewish	Calories per serving	Fat (Grams)	% Calories as fat
Glazed Chestnuts Chestnuts, sugar, margarine, broth	117	4	34
Honeyed Sprouts Brussels sprouts, honey	203	1	3
Humous Chick-peas, oil, olives, tahini	401	28	62
Iraqi Dried Fruit and Nut Salad Mixed dried fruit, raisins, sugar, pine nuts, almonds	420	8	17
Iraqi Minted Salad Cucumbers, tomatoes, radishes, onions, oil	143	14	86
Klops with Eggs Beef, broth, bread crumbs, onions, carrots, eggs	947	61	58
Kreplach Flour, eggs, beef, onions	40	1	27

JEWISH	Calories per serving	Fat (Grams)	% Calories as fat
Krupnik Broth, oil, onions, carrots, parsnips, mushrooms, tomatoes, barley, potatoes	272	6	19
Lamb in Spinach Leaves Lamb, spinach, onions, oil, tomato juice	454	27	54
Lemon Lamb Lamb, oil, onions, broth	537	29	48
Matzo Pudding Matzos, wine, margarine, dried fruit, walnuts, sugar, eggs	672	34	46
Milchige Soup Peas, potatoes, carrots, milk, sugar, onions, butter	209	10	42
Moroccan Beef and Olive Casserole Beef, oil, celery, olives	295	25	77
Mushroom Pilaf Rice, mushrooms, tomatoes, margarine	319	12	34

JEWISH	Calories per serving	Fat (Grams)	% Calories as fat
Orange Salad with Poppy Seeds Oranges, sugar, oil, poppy seeds	166	10	55
Peppers in Oil with Cheese Bell peppers, oil, cheese	431	39	81
Persian Almond Soup (*Marka Shkedim mi Paras*) Veal, eggs, almonds, celery, onions	674	50	66
Persian Cucumber Salad Cucumber, sugar, radishes, yogurt	49	1	22
Potato Kugel Potato, eggs, flour, chicken fat, onions	183	6	31
Potato Latkes Potatoes, flour, eggs, oil	241	11	41
Potato Salad Potatoes, oil, onions, mustard, mayonnaise	258	23	79

JEWISH	Calories per serving	Fat (Grams)	% Calories as fat
Prickly Pear Compote Prickly pear, sugar	181	1	5
Rice Souffle with Chicken Livers Rice, broth, chicken livers, flour, sherry, eggs, margarine	391	21	49
Salami Omelete Salami, eggs, oil	282	23	72
Sausage Pancakes (*Wurst Pfannkuchen*) Wurst, eggs, margarine	359	31	78
Sephardic Garlic Soup Garlic, oil, bread, milk	144	8	51
Sour Cream Borscht Beets, carrots, parsnips, celery, onions, tomatoes, sugar, wine, sour cream	120	6	47

JEWISH	Calories per serving	Fat (Grams)	% Calories as fat
Sour Cream Hamantaschen Yeast, milk, flour, eggs, sugar, sour cream, poppy seeds, walnuts, corn syrup, raisins, butter	196	8	34
Stuffed Eggs Eggs, margarine, bread crumbs, butter	186	16	77
Stuffed Onions Onions, lamb, oil, almonds, broth, bread crumbs	258	16	56
Sweet and Sour Meatballs Beef, onions, oil, eggs, flour, tomato puree, broth, sugar	409	25	56
Ukrainian Sauerkraut and Carrot Salad Sauerkraut, carrot, oil	105	7	59
Veal with Dumplings Veal, margarine, onions, carrot, celery, parsnip, bread crumbs, flour, egg, broth	578	34	53

JEWISH	Calories per serving	Fat (Grams)	% Calories as fat
Yemenite Yogurt Soup	106	7	60
Yogurt, cucumber, oil			

GERMAN
FOOD

Finding low-fat choices among German dishes is easier than for most of the cuisines in this book. But that doesn't mean that German cuisine is always low in fat. It has its share of dishes swimming in oil. For example, one of the most universally recognized German dishes, Schnitzel (veal cutlet), has 72 percent of its calories from fat and Hungarian Goulash, 79 percent. Though butter and cream are common ingredients in German cuisine, they are generally not used to excess. All of the Best Bets listed below provide 30 percent or less of their calories from fat. And there are several more dishes listed in these pages that provide a respectable 30 to 35 percent calories from fat.

GERMAN BEST BETS

Apple Rice • Apple Strudel • Buttermilk Soup • Cold Wine Soup • Dried Bean Salad • Glazed Chestnuts • Liver Patties • Noodle Pudding • Potato Dumplings • Semolina Pudding • Spatzle • Tapioca Souffle

GERMAN	Calories per serving	Fat (Grams)	% Calories as fat
Apple Rice (*Apfelreis mit Schneehaube*) Apples, rice, milk, butter, sugar, eggs, raisins	613	15	22
Apple Strudel (*Apfelstrudel*) Apples, flour, eggs, sugar, butter, bread crumbs, almonds, raisins	588	20	30
Baked Mushrooms with Noodles (*Pilzauflauf mit Nudeln*) Noodles, mushrooms, butter, bread crumbs	337	12	31
Bavarian Bread Dumplings (*Bayerisches Semmelklosse*) Rolls, milk, ham, eggs, onions	361	13	33
Bavarian Cabbage (*Bayerisches Kraut*) Cabbage, apples, butter, wine, sugar	165	6	33

GERMAN	Calories per serving	Fat (Grams)	% Calories as fat
Beef Goulash (*Rindergulasch*) Beef, onion, butter, flour, broth, tomatoes	481	36	67
Beer Soup (*Biersuppe*) Beer, flour, sugar, butter, eggs	164	6	31
Bread Pudding (*Brotpudding*) Bread, sugar, milk, butter, flour, raisins, candied fruit, almonds, rum	691	27	36
Buttermilk Soup (*Buttermilchsuppe*) Buttermilk, flour, bacon, onions, potatoes	211	5	20
Cabbage Rolls (*Krautwickel*) Cabbage, beef, pork, eggs, onions, butter, broth, flour, cream	453	27	54
Cabbage with Bacon (*Weisskraut mit Speck*) Cabbage, onions, potatoes, bacon	226	10	41

GERMAN	Calories per serving	Fat (Grams)	% Calories as fat
Carp with Horseradish (*Schleie mit Sahnemeerrettich*) Carp, horseradish, cream	517	34	60
Chicken Fricassee (*Hühnerfrikassee*) Chicken, butter, broth, flour, mushrooms, wine, egg yolks, cream	1138	83	65
Chicken Paprika (*Paprika Huhn*) Chicken, butter, onions, broth, cream	948	71	67
Cold Wine Soup (*Weinkaltschale*) Wine, raisins, semolina, eggs, sugar	221	3	12
Creamed Potatoes (*Rahmkartoffeln*) Potatoes, butter, flour, cream	334	19	52
Dried Bean Salad (*Kernbohnensalat*) White beans, broth, bacon	248	6	22

GERMAN	Calories per serving	Fat (Grams)	% Calories as fat
Egg Pudding with Spanish Sauce (*Eierauflauf*) Eggs, milk, butter, cream, flour, onions, broth	498	43	78
Farina Dumplings (*Griessklosschen*) Farina, milk, butter, eggs	151	10	57
Glazed Chestnuts (*Glasierte Kastanien*) Chestnuts, sugar, butter, gravy, broth	215	4	18
Goose Liver with Apples (*Ganseleber mit Apfeln*) Goose liver, flour, butter, apples, onion	207	8	36
Green Potato Soup (*Grune Kartoffelsuppe*) Potatoes, tomatoes, turnip, celery, onion, butter, flour, broth, sour cream, bread	208	8	34

GERMAN	Calories per serving	Fat (Grams)	% Calories as fat
Grilled Carp (*Karpfen, gegrillt*) Carp, lemon juice	254	13	44
Hazelnut Omelet (*Hazelnussomeletten*) Eggs, flour, milk, sugar, hazelnuts, butter	319	23	64
Hungarian Goulash (*Ungarischer Gulasch-Eintopf*) Beef, pork salt, onions, potatoes	906	74	74
Kasseler Roast Rib of Pork (*Kasseler Rippenspeer*) Pork roast, onion, tomato, celery, butter, flour, sour cream	659	39	53
Lamb Stew (*Hammelfleisch-Eintopt*) Lamb, mustard greens, potatoes, bacon, flour	533	20	33

German	Calories per serving	Fat (Grams)	% Calories as fat
Liver Patties (*Leberklosse, feine*) Liver, onion, butter, eggs, flour, cornmeal, broth	378	11	27
Liver Spatzle (*Leberspatzle*) Liver, flour, eggs, butter, onion	793	30	35
Meat and Bean Stew (*Bohnen-Eintopf*) Beef, onions, butter, green beans, potatoes	402	20	46
Noodle Pudding (*Nudelauflauf*) Noodles, eggs, butter, milk, sugar	525	16	27
Oatmeal Soup (*Haferflockensuppe*) Oats, egg yolks, butter	170	15	78
Paprika Cutlet with Cream (*Paprika-Rahmschnitzel*) Veal, butter, flour, cream	455	37	74

GERMAN	Calories per serving	Fat (Grams)	% Calories as fat
Parmesan Patties (*Kasecreme*) Milk, eggs, Parmesan cheese, cornstarch	213	13	56
Pike in Sour Cream (*Hecht in Sauren Rahm*) Pike, butter, wine, anchovies, bread crumbs, sour cream	475	24	45
Pork Chops with Apples (*Schweinnekoteletten mit Gebratenen Apfeln*) Pork chops, butter, apples	379	19	45
Pork Fillets (*Schweinefilet*) Pork, butter, onion, tomato, flour, broth, sour cream, wine	219	9	38
Pork Rolls (*Schweinerouladen*) Pork, onion, egg, roll, flour, butter, broth, mustard	878	63	65

GERMAN	Calories per serving	Fat (Grams)	% Calories as fat
Potato Dumplings (*Gekochte Kartoffelklosse*) Potatoes, flour, eggs, bread, butter	442	7	14
Potato Patties (*Kartoffelpastetchen*) Potatoes, milk, butter, roll, onion, veal, egg	347	15	39
Poultry Pie (*Geflugelpastete*) Chicken, flour, butter, eggs, cream, onion, cheese	695	49	63
Rice Pancakes (*Reisschmarren*) Rice, milk, butter, eggs, almonds, raisins, currants	522	29	50
Salzburg "Nockerln" (*Salzburger Nockerln*) Eggs, sugar, butter, brandy	188	8	40
Sauerbraten Beef, onions, oil, tomatoes, flour, butter, cream	401	26	58

GERMAN	Calories per serving	Fat (Grams)	% Calories as fat
Sauerkraut Cabbage, butter, onions, apples, potatoes, wine	220	9	37
Sauerkraut Salad (*Sauerkrautsalat*) Sauerkraut, oil, apples, onion, sugar	178	11	53
Schnitzel Stew (*Schnitzel-Eintopf*) Beef, onions, butter, carrots, potatoes, broth, cream, catsup, flour	732	39	47
Semolina Pudding **with Fruit Sauce** (*Griessflammeri*) Semolina, milk, sugar, butter, almonds, raisins, egg, strawberries, cornstarch, wine	464	8	15
Sole in White Wine (*Seezunge in Weisswein*) Sole, butter, wine, flour	382	14	33
Spatzle Flour, eggs	478	5	10

GERMAN	Calories per serving	Fat (Grams)	% Calories as fat
Spinach Pancakes (*Spinatpfannkuchen*) Spinach, eggs, flour, milk, butter	315	21	61
Spinach Pudding (*Spinatpudding*) Spinach, rolls, milk, onions, butter, eggs	290	18	57
Stuffed Apples (*Gefullte Apfel*) Apples, raisins, sugar, bread crumbs, nuts, butter, wine	376	14	34
Stuffed Cucumbers (*Gurken, gefullt*) Cucumbers, rolls, milk, butter, onion, eggs, bacon, broth	291	16	50
Stuffed Eggs (*Gefullte Eier*) Eggs, ham, anchovies, onions, oil	123	8	59
Tapioca Souffle (*Sagoauflauf*) Tapioca, milk, sugar, butter, eggs	432	15	30

GERMAN	Calories per serving	Fat (Grams)	% Calories as fat
Tomato Souffle (*Tommatenauflauf*) Tomatoes, milk, butter, flour, eggs	319	11	32
Tomatoes Nana (*Tomatoen Nana*) Tomatoes, chicken, walnuts, cream, mayonnaise	466	43	83
Turnip Stew (*Ruben-Eintopf*) Turnips, lamb, butter, tomatoes, flour, butter, broth	433	24	49
Veal Cutlet (*Schnitzel, naturell*) Veal, oil, butter	410	33	72
Veal Goulash (*Kalbsgulasch*) Veal, butter, onions, tomatoes, flour	385	28	65
Venison Loin (*Rehrucken*) Venison, milk, bacon, onion, butter, broth, sour cream, flour, cream, wine	224	17	67

GREEK FOOD

The subtle flavor of Greek dishes belies the presence of relatively large amounts of fat in its many recipes. On the plus side, the fat is usually heart-healthy olive oil—low in saturated and high in monounsaturated fats. On the negative side, olive oil still contains a hefty 120 calories per tablespoon. Vitamin C–rich tomato-based sauces are common—perfect for sopping up with low-fat hard breads. Most Greek recipes call for a variety of vegetables: lots of tomatoes, onions, and beans. Low-fat seafood is also a common ingredient.

Because of the added oil in Greek cooking, only

one of the Best Bets listed below provides 30 percent or less calories from fat—surprisingly, it's the Caramel Custard (25 percent calories from fat). The rest of the dishes listed below provide between 30 and 36 percent. Since the basic ingredients are healthful, all you need to do when preparing Greek food at home is cut back on the required olive oil and use the leanest cuts of meat to keep fat and calories to a minimum.

GREEK BEST BETS

Baked Beans, Plaki Style • *Bean Soup* • *Caramel Custard* • *Chicken Rice Soup Avgolemono* • *Chick-pea Soup, Thessaly Style* • *Green Beans Braised with Mint and Potatoes* • *Honey-Cheese Pie* • *Lamb with Artichokes and Dill* • *Lentil Soup* • *Tomatoes and Herbs with Rice*

GREEK	Calories per serving	Fat (Grams)	% Calories as fat
Almond Sponge Cake with Syrup (*Revani*) Semolina, flour, sugar, butter, eggs, almonds, brandy	287	14	45
Artichokes and Green Peas (*Anginares me Araka*) Artichokes, peas, flour, onion, tomato sauce, sugar, oil	282	19	59
Baked Beans, Plaki Style (*Fassolia Plaki*) Dried beans, onions, garlic, oil, tomatoes, carrots, celery	297	11	34
Baked Shrimp and Feta (*Garides Kokkiyia me Feta*) Shrimp, onion, butter, tomato sauce, tomatoes, feta cheese, garlic	355	16	40

GREEK	Calories per serving	Fat (Grams)	% Calories as fat
Baklava (Pastry) Sugar, honey, nuts, butter, filo pastry	142	8	49
Bean Soup (*Fassoulada*) Dried beans, onions, carrots, tomatoes, oil	300	11	33
Braised Potatoes, Peloponnesos Style (*Patates Yiahni*) Potatoes, oil, onions, tomatoes	237	11	42
Butter Cookies (*Kourabiedes*) Butter, sugar, nuts, flour, whiskey, almonds	110	7	54
Caramel Custard (*Crema Caramella*) Sugar, milk, eggs	214	6	26
Cheese Souffle (*Souffle Tyri*) Feta cheese, butter, flour, milk, eggs	228	17	68

GREEK	Calories per serving	Fat (Grams)	% Calories as fat
Chicken Rice Soup Avgolemono (*Soupa Avgolemono*) Broth, rice, eggs, butter	126	5	34
Chicken Sauteed with Tomatoes and Rice (*Kota Atzem Pilafi Ipiriotiko*) Chicken, butter, onion, tomato sauce, rice	643	29	41
Chick-pea Soup, Thessaly Style (*Revithia Soupa Thessalias*) Chick-peas, onions, oil	335	13	36
Chicken with Okra (*Kota Me Bamia*) Chicken, okra, butter, onion, tomato sauce	413	24	52
Crispy Cheese Squares (*Tyropita Trifti Thrakis*) [Appetizer] Butter, oil, milk, cheese, flour	30	2	69

GREEK	Calories per serving	Fat (Grams)	% Calories as fat
Eggplant Moussaka (*Melitzanes Moussaka*) Eggplant, oil, onions, lamb, wine, tomato sauce, bread crumbs, eggs, white sauce, Parmesan cheese	515	30	52
Eggplant Stuffed with Aromatics (*Imam Bayaldi*) Eggplant, oil, onions, tomatoes, garlic, sugar	189	13	61
Eggplant Stuffing (*Kima Apo Melitzannes*) Eggplant, oil, onions, garlic, wine, tomato paste, bread crumbs	111	7	58
Fish, Plaki Style (*Psari Plaki*) Fish, oil, onion, wine, tomatoes, celery, carrots, spinach, garlic	501	34	61
Fish Stew (*Bourtheto*) Fish, oil, onions	468	31	60

GREEK	Calories per serving	Fat (Grams)	% Calories as fat
Fish, Stifado Style (*Psari Stifado*) Fish, oil, tomato juice, wine, sugar, onions, garlic	396	21	49
Fish Roe Salad (*Taramosalata*) Potatoes, fish roe, oil, onions	266	24	82
Fish Soup with Vegetables Cretan Style (*Psarosoupa me Horta Kritiki*) Fish, oil, onions, carrots, celery, tomatoes, zucchini, flour	228	14	56
Fish Soup Patmos Style (*Psarosoupa Patmou*) Fish, onions, celery, oil, potatoes, rice, tomatoes	630	26	37
Fried Cheese (*Saganaki*) Feta cheese, butter	122	11	81

GREEK	Calories per serving	Fat (Grams)	% Calories as fat
Green Beans Braised with Mint and Potatoes (*Fassolakia me Patates Moraitika*) Green beans, potatoes, oil, margarine, tomato juice	128	6	39
Hand-Rolled Biscuits (*Koulourakia*) Butter, flour, sugar, eggs, cream, cognac	48	2	36
Herbed Yogurt and Cucumber (*Tzatziki*) Yogurt, cucumber, garlic, oil	107	5	39
Honey-Cheese Pie (*Melopita*) Cottage cheese, honey, sugar, eggs, flour, butter	235	8	31
Honey-Dipped Cookies (*Finikia*) Butter, oil, sugar, orange juice, flour, nuts, honey	205	11	48

GREEK	Calories per serving	Fat (Grams)	% Calories as fat
Lamb with Artichokes and Dill (*Arni me Anginares Kai Anithon*) Lamb, oil, onions, tomatoes, tomato paste, artichokes	392	15	35
Lamb with Vegetables and Herbs (*Arni Fikasee*) Lamb, oil, onions, garlic, carrots, celery, margarine, flour	622	34	49
Lentil Soup (*Faki*) Lentils, onion, garlic, celery, tomatoes, oil	191	7	35
Lima Beans with Yogurt (*Koukia me Yaourti*) Lima beans, oil, onions, sugar, yogurt	177	8	38
Octopus with Dressing (*Oktapodi me Ladoxido*) Octopus, oil	208	15	65

GREEK	Calories per serving	Fat (Grams)	% Calories as fat
Okra Braised with Tomato and Parsley (*Bamyes Yiahni*) Okra, oil, onions, tomatoes, sugar	161	12	68
Pickled Mushrooms (*Manitaria Tursi*) Mushrooms, oil	119	11	84
Pork Braised with Celery (*Hirino Selino Avgolemono*) Pork, butter, onions, celery, flour, eggs	797	52	59
Pork Braised with Wine and Coriander (*Hirino Riganato*) Pork, garlic, wine, tomato sauce	422	26	56
Potato-Garlic Sauce (*Skordalia*) Potatoes, oil, garlic	186	17	80
Quince Preserves (*Kydoni Glyko*) Quinces, sugar, almonds	114	<1	<8

GREEK	Calories per serving	Fat (Grams)	% Calories as fat
Rice Pudding (*Rizogalo*) Milk, rice, sugar, butter, eggs	424	18	37
Chicken and Broth (*Kota Kai Zomos*) Chicken, onions, leeks, celery, carrots, tomatoes, tomato paste, butter, oil	402	22	49
Spinach and Rice (*Spanakorizo*) Spinach, rice, oil, onion, tomato sauce	95	4	38
Spinach Pie (*Spanakopita*) Spinach, oil, onions, feta cheese, eggs, flour, butter	394	28	64
Squid Baked with Rice (*Kalamarakia Pilafi*) Squid, rice, oil, garlic, wine, tomatoes, butter	485	23	43

GREEK	Calories per serving	Fat (Grams)	% Calories as fat
Stuffed Grapevine Leaves (*Dolmades Yialandzi*) Oil, onion, garlic, rice, grapevine leaves	35	3	65
Summer Vegetable Soup (*Hortosoupa Kalokerini*) Butter, onion, carrot, celery, okra, beans, squash, tomatoes, broth	83	5	55
Swordfish on Skewers (*Xifias Souvlakia*) Swordfish, oil, tomatoes, bell peppers	361	18	46
Tomato Salad with Feta Cheese (*Domatosalata me Feta*) Tomatoes, oil, feta cheese	357	33	82
Tomatoes and Herbs with Rice (*Bourani*) Tomatoes, oil, tomato juice, garlic, rice	417	14	31

GREEK	Calories per serving	Fat (Grams)	% Calories as fat
Tomatoes Stuffed with Meat and Rice (*Domates Yemistes me Kima Kai Rizi*) Tomatoes, oil, onions, garlic, lamb, wine, rice	201	9	39
Veal and Macaroni (*Pastitsada Korfiatiki*) Veal, oil, onions, garlic, wine, tomato, macaroni, butter, Parmesan cheese	827	42	46
Veal, Thracian Style (*Stamnaki*) Veal, garlic, onions, bell pepper, cheese, oil, tomatoes, flour	469	28	53
Walnut Syrup Sponge Cake (*Karydopita*) Zwieback, walnuts, eggs, sugar, cognac	340	16	43
Whipped Eggplant Salad (*Melitzanosalata*) Eggplant, garlic, tomatoes, oil	161	15	81

GREEK	Calories per serving	Fat (Grams)	% Calories as fat
Zucchini Souffle (*Souffle Kolokithakia*) Zucchini, butter, flour, milk, Parmesan cheese, eggs	358	25	62

CAJUN FOOD

South Louisiana, otherwise known as "Cajun country," is the home of Cajun cuisine. Up until recently, you had to take a trip to the South to get a taste of the real thing, but because of the recent increase in popularity of Cajun cooking, Cajun restaurants are popping up all over the country. But before you run out to taste-test the food, there are a few things you need to know.

The hallmark of Cajun cuisine is fat—and lots of it. Butter and lard figure prominently into most recipes. Even dishes that begin with low-calorie ingredients such as seafood and vegetables usually have butter, margarine, and/or lard added to make them high-fat dishes in the end. In addition to having fat-laden ingredients, several dishes are also deep-fried. And traditional serving sizes are enormous. Put them all together and you have a high-fat, high-cholesterol, high-calorie cuisine. But there are a few exceptions. The Best Bets for Cajun are provided below. Not all are ideal (30 percent or less calories from fat) but if you're eating Cajun they are the lesser evils. The exact calorie and fat counts for these and other Cajun dishes are in the following pages.

Because the serving sizes of many dishes tend to be big enough for two or three people, order one and share with someone. It won't change the percentage of fat in the dish, but it will cut your total fat and calorie intake.

Cutting fat and calories in Cajun dishes you prepare at home is easy. With low-fat seafood and vegetables as the basis of most recipes, simply use half the fat the recipe calls for (or less), and when a recipe says it serves four, count on serving six to eight.

CAJUN BEST BETS

Baked Fresh Fish with Crabmeat Gravy
• Beans with Sausage and Cajun Rice •
Cajun Rice • Candied Yams •
Cornbread (without butter) • Crawfish
Boudin • Fish Sauce Piquant • Lemon
Coffee Cake • Shrimp and Crabmeat
Jambalaya • Shrimp and Crabmeat
Spaghetti • Smothered Potatoes • Spicy
Tomatoes

CAJUN	Calories per serving	Fat (Grams)	% Calories as fat
Baked Chicken (*Poule Rotie*) Chicken, onions, oil, bell peppers, celery, broth, parsley	752	55	66
Baked Fresh Fish with Crabmeat Gravy (*Poisson Frais Roti avec une Sauce Rouge de Viande de Crabe*) Fish, oil, onions, tomatoes, broth, bell peppers, crabmeat, butter, garlic	494	14	26
Baked Pork Chops with Onion Gravy and Rice Pork chops, margarine, onions, broth, rice, garlic	1006	64	57
Beans with Sausage and Cajun Rice (*Feves Caille Seches avec Andouille*) Pinto beans, broth, sausage, onions, bell peppers, sugar, garlic, rice	959	39	37

CAJUN	Calories per serving	Fat (Grams)	% Calories as fat
Beignets (Doughnuts) Flour, milk, oil, egg, sugar	77	4	46
Biscuits Flour, sugar, oil, butter	264	12	41
Black-eyed Peas with Bacon and Ham (*Feves de Black-eye avec Bequine et Tasso*) Black-eyed peas, broth, bacon, ham, onions, bell peppers, celery, garlic	385	17	41
Blackened Chicken Chicken, butter	390	25	58
Blackened Redfish Fish, butter	533	36	61
Bouilli with Rice (Cajun soup) Beef ribs, sirloin, heart, spleen, kidney, liver, flour, oil, onions, bell peppers, broth, rice, garlic	1096	54	44

CAJUN	Calories per serving	Fat (Grams)	% Calories as fat
Bread Pudding (*Poudine au Pain*) Bread, butter, sugar, evaporated milk, eggs	384	20	46
Butter Beans (*Feves Plattes Fraiches*) Butter beans, butter, broth, lard, onions, garlic, sugar	412	26	57
Cabbage Rolls (each) (*Rouleaux de Chou*) Cabbage, ground beef, onions, butter, tomato sauce, bell peppers, celery, broth, garlic	258	18	62
Cajun Fried Catfish (*Barbue Frit*) Catfish, egg, milk, corn flour, lard, mustard	286	13	40
Cajun Macaroni Salad (*Salade de Macaroni*) Macaroni, mayonnaise, onions, bell peppers, eggs	577	49	77

CAJUN	Calories per serving	Fat (Grams)	% Calories as fat
Cajun Rice Rice, broth, butter, onions, celery, bell pepper	134	2	13
Cajun Rice and Shrimp Shrimp, rice, onions, butter, mushrooms, broth, bell peppers	474	25	47
Candied Yams (*Patates Douces en Candi*) Sweet potatoes, brown sugar, butter	384	7	15
Carrot, Apple, and Raisin Salad (*Salade de Carotte, Pomme, et Raisin*) Apples, carrots, raisins, mayonnaise	280	22	72

Cajun	Calories per serving	Fat (Grams)	% Calories as fat
Chicken and Okra Gumbo (*Gombo de Poule et Gombo Fevi*) Fried chicken, okra, tomato sauce, flour, broth, onions, bell peppers, celery, sausage, ham, eggs, rice	1293	87	61
Chicken Chartres (Baked Chicken with Fried Potatoes) Chicken, onions, butter, potatoes, bacon, ham, broth, eggs, bearnaise sauce	1416	107	68
Chicken Sauce Piquant (*Sauce Piquante de Poule*) Chicken, oil, broth, onions, bell pepper, garlic, butter, celery, tomato sauce, catsup, rice	926	57	55
Cornbread Flour, cornmeal, sugar, corn flour, milk, butter, eggs	347	13	34

CAJUN	Calories per serving	Fat (Grams)	% Calories as fat
Cornbread Dressing Giblets, butter, onions, celery, bell peppers, cornbread, evaporated milk, eggs, margarine, garlic, broth	301	14	43
Country Steak and Gravy with Rice (*Steak et Sauce de Campagne*) Steak, broth, oil, onions, bell peppers, parsley, rice, flour	699	35	45
Couche-Couche with Cane Syrup (Breakfast dish) Cornmeal, oil, milk, syrup	390	16	36
Crawfish Boudin (*Boudin d'Ecrevisses [Crawfish Sausage]*) Crawfish, onions, parsley, oil, rice	183	6	31

Cajun	Calories per serving	Fat (Grams)	% Calories as fat
Crawfish Boulettes (*Boulettes d'Ecrevisses [Fried Crawfish Balls]*) Crawfish, butter, onions, bell peppers, parsley, potatoes, eggs, flour, milk, bread crumbs	99	5	47
Crawfish Etouffee with Rice (*Etouffee d'Ecrevisses*) Crawfish, onions, flour, celery, bell peppers, catsup, broth, rice, oil, margarine, garlic	490	24	44
Cream Cheese and Roasted Pecan Cookies (*Tit Gateaux de Creme de Fromage et Pacanes Grillees*) Flour, butter, sugar, egg, cream cheese, pecans, cocoa	118	8	60

CAJUN	Calories per serving	Fat (Grams)	% Calories as fat
Eggplant, Corn, and Cheese Casserole (*Casserole de Breme, Mais, et Fromage*) Eggplant, eggs, corn, onions, bell peppers, butter, garlic, cheese, cracker crumbs	335	23	63
Eggplant and Crabmeat Casserole with Cheese Sauce (*Casserole de Breme et Crabe avec une Sauce de Fromage*) Eggplant, butter, onions, mushrooms, bell peppers, celery, broth, bread crumbs, crab, flour, cheese, evaporated milk, garlic	680	48	64
Fish Sauce Piquant with Rice (*Sauce Piquante de Poisson*) Fish, onions, oil, bell peppers, celery, garlic, tomato sauce, broth, flour, rice	520	13	22

Cajun	Calories per serving	Fat (Grams)	% Calories as fat
Fresh Coconut Pralines (*Pralines au Coco Frais*) Coconut, sugar, evaporated milk, butter	227	9	34
Fresh Fish in Brown Gravy (*Poisson Frais dans une Sauce Rouillee*) Fish, flour, onions, rice, broth, oil	728	38	47
Fried Chicken (*Poulet Frit*) Chicken, flour, eggs, evaporated milk, oil	857	61	64
Fried Crawfish (*Ecrevisses Frites*) Crawfish, evaporated milk, egg, corn flour, oil	401	15	33
Greasy Rice (*Riz a la Graisse*) Rice, bacon, oil, eggs	223	10	38

Cajun	Calories per serving	Fat (Grams)	% Calories as fat
Ground Beef, Smoked Sausage, and Cabbage Jambalaya	848	41	43
Beef, sausage, oil, onions, celery, parsley, tomatoes, cabbage, broth, rice, bell peppers, garlic			
Hot Cajun Rice and Shrimp	474	25	47
Shrimp, rice, broth, butter, onions, bell peppers, mushrooms, garlic			
Hush Puppies (each) (*Boules de Pain de Mais*)	48	1	21
Flour, cornmeal, sugar, onions, bell pepper, egg			
Lemon Coffee Cake (*Tit Gateau de Limon*)	295	13	39
Flour, butter, sugar, eggs, cornstarch			

Cajun	Calories per serving	Fat (Grams)	% Calories as fat
Marinated and Smothered Grillades in Rusty Gravy with Rice (*Grillades Amarinees et Etouffees*) Pork, oil, onions, rice, garlic	1364	93	62
Oyster Dressing Bread crumbs, onions, celery, bell peppers, margarine, parsley, butter, garlic, oysters	334	21	58
Potato Stew with Smoked Sausage (*Fricassee de Patate Anglaise et Andouille*) Sausage, potatoes, broth, butter, onions, flour, margarine	810	42	47
Rice and Mirliton Dressing (*Farre de Riz et Mirliton*) Mirlitons (chayotes), pork, onions, oil, beef, celery, bell peppers, broth, parsley, rice	318	15	42

Cajun	Calories per serving	Fat (Grams)	% Calories as fat
Roasted Pecan Butter Pecan Pie (*Tarte de Pacanes Grillees Faite en Beurre*) Flour, butter, pecans, eggs, sugar, corn syrup	564	29	47
Roasted Pecan Cake with Roasted Pecan Filling (*Gateau de Pacanes Grillees avec Pacanes pour Mettre entre Ton Gateau*) Flour, sugar, butter, milk, eggs, pecans, sweetened condensed milk, cream cheese, cream	581	26	40
Shrimp and Crabmeat Jambalaya (*Jambalaya de Chevrettes et Viande de Crabe*) Shrimp, butter, tomato sauce, onions, bell peppers, parsley, broth, crabmeat, rice, garlic	514	16	27

Cajun	Calories per serving	Fat (Grams)	% Calories as fat
Shrimp and Crabmeat Spaghetti (*Macaroni avec Chevrettes et Viande de Crabe*) Shrimp, crabmeat, butter, onions, bell peppers, celery, tomato sauce, broth, catsup, oil, spaghetti, garlic	668	21	28
Shrimp and Okra Gumbo (*Gombo de Chevrettes et Gombo Fevi*) Shrimp, onions, bell peppers, oil, flour, okra, tomatoes, broth, garlic	372	22	52
Shrimp Etouffee with Rice (*Etouffee de Chevrettes*) Shrimp, butter, onions, celery, bell peppers, parsley, broth, rice, tomato paste	423	20	42

Cajun	Calories per serving	Fat (Grams)	% Calories as fat
Shrimp Fricassee with Rice (*Fricassee de Chevrettes*) Shrimp, onions, broth, bell peppers, oil, flour, rice, garlic	571	24	38
Smoked Sausage Dressing Sausage, bread crumbs, broth, butter, onions, celery, bell peppers, margarine, garlic	415	28	61
Smoked Sausage in Red Gravy with Rice (*Andouille dans une Sauce Rouge*) Sausage, broth, butter, onions, celery, bell peppers, tomato sauce, parsley, rice, garlic	974	68	63
Smothered Okra and Tomatoes (*Gombo Fevi et Tomates Etouffes*) Okra, tomatoes, lard, onions, bell peppers, celery, garlic	225	15	60

Cajun	Calories per serving	Fat (Grams)	% Calories as fat
Smothered Potatoes (*Patates Etouffees*) Potatoes, oil, onions, broth	255	9	30
Spicy Tomatoes [1 cup] Tomatoes, onions, hot peppers, garlic	49	1	9
Stuffed Beef Roast (*Roti de Viande de Bete Piqure a l'Ail*) Beef roast, onions, bell peppers, broth, butter, garlic	617	38	55
Stuffed Pork Pot Roast with Rice (*Roti de Cochon Piqure a l'Ail*) Pork roast, broth, lard, butter, onions, rice, garlic, bell pepper	930	37	35
Stuffed Smothered Steak (*Steak Piqure a l'Ail et Etouffe*) Steak, broth, onion, bell peppers, rice, garlic, sugar, mustard, flour	778	38	44

CAJUN	Calories per serving	Fat (Grams)	% Calories as fat
Sweet Potato Omelet	365	21	51
Eggs, sweet potatoes, brown sugar, potatoes, eggs, evaporated milk, chicken fat, ham, onions, bell peppers, yellow squash, zucchini, peas, oil			
Yeast Rolls (*Pain de Froment*)	183	8	39
Flour, butter, sugar, yeast			

JAPANESE FOOD

Of the fifteen international cuisines in this book, Japanese has the largest selection of low-fat dishes. With the exception of a few deep-fried dishes, most are exceptionally low in fat. Seafood is the focus of many Japanese dishes. You'll also find generous servings of vegetables as part of main dishes in Japanese food, as in other Oriental cuisines. The only negative to Japanese foods is the high level of sodium generally found. Soy sauce is both a standard ingredient and condiment. It provides 1029 milligrams of sodium per tablespoon, so if sodium is a concern, you should avoid it.

Sushi is generally low in fat, but the amount of fat varies depending on what type of seafood is used. Soups are an excellent low-fat choice at Japanese restaurants. They consist of little more than broth with miso, vegetables, and sometimes chicken or beef. There are more Japanese dishes than the ones listed below that are equally low in fat and calories.

JAPANESE BEST BETS

Beef and New Potato Stew • Chicken and Noodles in Miso-Thickened Soup • Chicken in Grilled Rice Cake Soup • Clams and Scallions in Bean Soup • Fish and Noodle Casserole • Glaze-Grilled Scallops • Peas and Rice • Pine-Cone Squid • Pork and Noodles in a Soy-Flavored Broth • Red Rice and Beans • Crab Sushi • Shrimp in Rice Cake Soup • Sweet Simmered Oriental Vegetables

JAPANESE	Calories per serving	Fat (Grams)	% Calories as fat
Beans and Assorted Vegetables (*Gomoku Mame Ni*) Soybeans, mushrooms, carrots, kelp, broth, soy sauce, sugar, *mirin* (syrupy rice wine)	126	4	26
Beef and New Potato Stew (*Guyniku To Shinjagaimo No Ni Mono*) Sirloin, potatoes, snow peas, broth, sugar, soy sauce, sake	417	6	13
Braised Beef with Vegetables (*Sukiyaki*) Sirloin, leeks, cabbage, collard greens, mushrooms, soy sauce, sake, broth, sugar, eggs	323	14	39
Braised Celery Strips (*Sengiri Nitsuke'*) Pork, sake, celery, sesame seeds, oil, soy sauce, sugar	79	5	57

JAPANESE	Calories per serving	Fat (Grams)	% Calories as fat
Braised Chicken Cubes and Vegetables (*Iri-dori*) Chicken, oil, carrot, soy sauce, sugar, sake	178	5	23
Braised Eggplant in Sesame and Bean Sauce (*Nasu No Rikyu Ni*) Eggplant, oil, broth, miso, sugar, sake, sesame seeds	206	11	48
Braised Japanese White Radish (*Daikon No Itame Ni*) Radishes, oil, broth, sugar, sake, soy sauce	67	2	23
Chicken and Noodles in Miso-Thickened Soup (*Miso Aji Ramen*) Soba noodles, broth, miso, chicken, green onions, sesame seeds	399	4	8

JAPANESE	Calories per serving	Fat (Grams)	% Calories as fat
Chicken and Potato Soup (*Satsuma-jiru*) Chicken, sake, potatoes, radishes, carrot, miso, *mirin* (syrupy rice wine), turnips	234	8	30
Chicken and Vegetable Pot with Dark Broth (*Tori Nabe'*) Chicken, green onions, leeks, bean curd, spinach, broth, soy sauce, *mirin* (syrupy rice wine), sugar, mushrooms	210	2	10
Chicken in Grilled Rice Cake Soup (*Tori Zoni*) Chicken, sake, rice cakes, broth, mushrooms, carrots, snow peas	374	2	4

JAPANESE	Calories per serving	Fat (Grams)	% Calories as fat
Clams and Scallions in Bean Soup (*Hamaguri No Miso Wan*) Kelp, soy sauce, green onion, clams, sake, miso	78	2	19
Cold Egg Custard (*Tamago-dofu*) Eggs, broth, *mirin* (syrupy rice wine), sugar, green onions	72	4	53
Cold Steamed Chicken (*Tori No Saka Mushi*) Chicken, sake, tomato, cucumber, sugar, soy sauce, oil	146	2	12
Crab Sushi (*Kani Chirashi-zushi*) Crabmeat, rice, ginger, sesame seeds, lotus root, mushrooms, snow peas	416	5	10
Egg Drop Soup (*Tamago Toji*) Broth, mushrooms, egg, soy sauce	25	1	32

JAPANESE	Calories per serving	Fat (Grams)	% Calories as fat
Fish and Noodle Casserole (*Shiromi No Soba Mushi*) Sole, soba noodles, broth, soy sauce, *mirin* (syrupy rice wine), sugar, green onions	173	2	8
Fish Steaks (*Kirimi*) Salmon, radishes	157	7	39
Garnished Rice with Tea (*Ocha-zuke'*) Rice, sesame seeds, coriander, tea	143	<1	1
Gingery Pork Saute (*Shoga Yaki*) Pork, ginger, sake, soy sauce, snow peas, oil	207	13	56
Gingery Rice Porridge (*Ozosui*) Broth, soy sauce, rice, chicken, mushrooms, collard greens, egg, ginger	169	4	21

JAPANESE	Calories per serving	Fat (Grams)	% Calories as fat
Glazed Beef Rolls (*Negi Maki*) Beef, green onions, oil, soy sauce, sugar, sake, broth, sesame seeds	43	2	50
Glazed Grilled Chicken Wings (*Teba Niku No Teri Yaki*) Chicken wings, soy sauce, *mirin* (syrupy rice wine), sugar	468	29	56
Glazed Grilled Eel (*Kabayaki*) Eel, soy sauce, sake, sugar	261	13	46
Glaze-Grilled Scallops (*Hotategai No Teri Yaki*) Scallops, sake, soy sauce, *mirin* (syrupy rice wine), sugar	128	1	4

Japanese	Calories per serving	Fat (Grams)	% Calories as fat
Glossy Pork and Pumpkin Stew (*Butaniku To Kabocha No Tsuya Ni*) Pork, oil, broth, sugar, sake, pumpkin, soy sauce, *mirin* (syrupy rice wine)	393	15	35
Japanese Vegetables in Dark Bean Soup (*Name'ko Iri No Miso Shiru*) Mushrooms, broth, soy sauce, miso, tofu, coriander	68	1	16
Mackerel in Bean Sauce (*Saba No Miso Ni*) Mackerel, kelp, ginger, miso, sugar, sake	270	12	39
Mackerel Loaves (*Saba-zushi*) Mackerel, sugar, soy sauce, rice, kelp	420	14	30

JAPANESE	Calories per serving	Fat (Grams)	% Calories as fat
Oriental Pork Pot Roast (*Butaniku No Maru Ni*) Pork, oil, soy sauce, sake, ginger, green onions	347	17	45
Oyster Pot with Bean Broth (*Kaki Nabe'*) Oysters, tofu, leeks, collard greens, kelp, miso, sugar, sake, ginger	156	3	15
Parent and Child Bowl (*Oyako Domburi*) Chicken, onion, broth, soy sauce, sugar, sake, eggs, coriander, rice	332	6	17
Peas and Rice (*Mame' Gohan*) Peas, rice, *mirin* (syrupy rice wine), sesame seeds	252	1	2

JAPANESE	Calories per serving	Fat (Grams)	% Calories as fat
Pine-Cone Squid (*Ika No Matsukasa Yaki*) Squid, soy sauce, *mirin* (syrupy rice wine), black sesame seeds	104	1	12
Pork and Bean Curd in Light Bean Soup (*Ton-jiru*) Pork, kelp, soy sauce, sake, miso, tofu, green onion	100	4	34
Pork and Noodles in a Soy-Flavored Broth (*Shoyu Aji Ramen*) Soba noodles, spinach, broth, pork	454	7	14
Pork and Vegetable Pot with Clear Broth (*Mizutaki*) Pork, bean curd, green onions, mushrooms, carrots, cabbage, dandelion greens, soy sauce, radishes, red pepper, kelp	276	11	36

JAPANESE	Calories per serving	Fat (Grams)	% Calories as fat
Pork Cutlet Omelet on Rice (*Katsudon*) Broth, soy sauce, sugar, sake, pork cutlets, eggs, coriander, rice	395	12	28
Red Rice and Beans (*Sekihan*) Red beans, rice, black sesame seeds	136	< 1	2
Rice Ovals Topped with Salmon (*Nigiri-zushi*) Rice, smoked salmon	65	1	19
Salt-Grilled Chicken Breast (*Tori Niku No Shio Yaki*) Chicken, sake	127	2	11
Sea Greens and Bean Curd in Light Bean Soup (*Wakame' To Tofu No Miso Shiru*) Kelp, broth, soy sauce, miso, tofu	71	1	16

JAPANESE	Calories per serving	Fat (Grams)	% Calories as fat
Shrimp in Rice Cake Soup (*Ebi Zoni*) Mushrooms, broth, soy sauce, shrimp, spinach, rice cakes	298	1	2
Silver Boats (*Gin-gami Mushi*) Shrimp, chicken, mushrooms, kelp, soy sauce, sake	85	1	13
Skewered Chicken Grill (*Yaki Tork*) Chicken, chicken livers, green onions, soy sauce, sugar, sake, *mirin* (syrupy rice wine)	261	9	32
Skewered Salt-Grilled Shrimps (*Ebi No Kushi Yaki*) Shrimp, sake, soy sauce	166	2	13

JAPANESE	Calories per serving	Fat (Grams)	% Calories as fat
Skillet-Grilled Beefsteaks and Vegetables (*Teppan Yaki*) Rib steaks, bell peppers, bean sprouts, oil, soy sauce, broth, radishes, red pepper	390	23	53
Snake's Eyes Soup (*Janome'-jiru*) Shrimp, soy sauce, sake, broth	117	2	12
Spicy Braised Livers (*Reba No Tsukuda Ni*) Chicken livers, green onions, oil, sake, *mirin* (syrupy rice wine), soy sauce, sugar	127	5	38
Spicy Stir-Fried Noodles (*Yaki Soba*) Soba noodles, pork, oil, cabbage, sake	411	14	30

JAPANESE	Calories per serving	Fat (Grams)	% Calories as fat
Steamed Egg Pudding (*Chawan Mushi*) Eggs, broth, soy sauce, *mirin* (syrupy rice wine), shrimp, chicken, mushrooms, snow peas	107	4	34
Stewed Turnips and Chicken Balls (*Kokabu To Toriniku Dango*) Mushrooms, chicken, egg, cornstarch, ginger, sake, sugar, soy sauce, turnips, spinach, broth	115	2	15
Sweet and Sour Sauce (*Amazu*) [per ½ cup] Sugar, vinegar	193	0	0
Sweet Rice Porridge with Red Beans (*Okayu*) Red beans, rice, rice cakes, sugar	440	< 1	1

JAPANESE	Calories per serving	Fat (Grams)	% Calories as fat
Sweet Simmered Oriental Vegetables (*Uma Ni*) Mushrooms, carrots, bamboo shoots, broth, sake, sugar, soy sauce, *mirin* (syrupy rice wine)	49	<1	2
Thick Sweet Omelet (*Atsu Yaki Tamago*) Broth, sugar, eggs, soy sauce, sake, oil, radishes	192	12	57
Turnip Clouds (*Kabura Mushi*) Broth, shrimp, turnips, egg white, soy sauce, sake, cornstarch	68	1	11
Vegetables in Rice Cake Soup (*Miso Zoni*) Broth, soy sauce, radishes, carrots, bamboo shoots, miso, dandelion greens, rice cakes	314	<1	1

JAPANESE	Calories per serving	Fat (Grams)	% Calories as fat
Vegetables and Seasoned Rice (*Kayaku Gohan*) Bean curd, bamboo shoots, carrot, rice, soy sauce, *mirin* (syrupy rice wine), oil	365	1	2
White Turnips in Dark Bean Soup (*Kokabu No Miso Shiru*) Turnips, turnip greens, broth, miso, soy sauce	39	0	0

INDIAN
FOOD

Because vegetarian dishes are abundant in Indian cuisine, making low-fat choices is relatively easy. Everyday vegetables eaten in the United States are transformed into exotic dishes by the wonderful combinations of spices traditional in Indian cooking. But you should still proceed with caution. The amount of oil used even in vegetarian curries varies greatly and can transform a low-calorie, low-fat dish into a dieter's disaster. Generally speaking, however, vegetarian Indian dishes are better bets than meat dishes. Steer clear of coconut milk and cream-based dishes, which are also common. They, too, are high in fat. If a creamy dish is what you're hungry for, opt instead for yogurt-based dishes. Traditional Indian dishes call for whole-milk yogurt, but it's still lower in fat than coconut milk. If you make the dish at home, substitute low-fat or non-fat yogurt. Vegetarian soups like lentil or split pea and baked bread (Naan) are good ways to start your meal.

INDIAN BEST BETS

Chick-peas and Spinach Marinade • Curried Chick-peas • Fruit Salad with Thickened Milk • Lentils and Vegetables with Chicken • Lentils and Spinach • Mango Fool • Naan • Onion Salad • Pineapple Fruit Salad • Rice and Chicken Pilaf • Rice Pilaf with Peas • Rice with Chick-peas

INDIAN	Calories per serving	Fat (Grams)	% Calories as fat
Beef Cooked in Coconut Milk (*Shakuti*) Beef, coconut milk, oil, onions, garlic, tamarind	539	48	80
Beef Curry (*Korma*) Beef, oil, onions, chili peppers, yogurt, garlic	330	21	58
Carrot Nut Pudding (*Gajar Ka Halva*) Carrots, milk, cream, honey, butter, raisins, almonds	365	21	52
Cauliflower with Carrots and Potatoes (*Puri Phulgobi*) Cauliflower, carrots, potatoes, oil, onions, garlic, tomatoes	183	9	45
Chapati Flour, oil	105	4	34

INDIAN	Calories per serving	Fat (Grams)	% Calories as fat
Chicken Stewed in Coconut Milk with Vegetables (*Murgi Ka Stew*) Chicken, coconut milk, lentils, potatoes, carrots, turnips, peas, oil, mangoes, onions, garlic, chili peppers	607	38	57
Chicken Vindaloo (*Murgh Vindaloo*) Chicken, garlic, molasses, potatoes, oil, onions, tomatoes, chili peppers	401	19	42
Chick-peas and Spinach Marinade (*Chana Palak Salaad*) Chick-peas, spinach, garlic, oil, honey	196	4	19
Chutney with Yogurt (*Mariyal Chutney*) Lentils, oil, yogurt, coconut, chili pepper	149	10	58
Cornmeal Bread (*Makkay Ki Roti*) Cornmeal, onions, butter	236	8	31

INDIAN	Calories per serving	Fat (Grams)	% Calories as fat
Cream-Stuffed Meatball Curry (*Malai Kofta*) Beef, sour cream, oil, tomatoes, yogurt, chili peppers	291	18	55
Curried Asparagus (*Asparagus Bhaji*) Asparagus, oil	97	8	73
Curried Bananas with Coconut (*Kaila Bhaji*) Bananas, soy sauce, oil, chili peppers, coconut, watercress, ginger, garlic	195	9	40
Curried Cheese and Peas (*Matar Panir*) Peas, tomatoes, powdered milk, oil, onions, yogurt, garlic	297	13	40
Curried Chick-peas (*Sukha Kala Chana*) Chick-peas, oil, onions, garlic, ginger, chilies	252	7	25

INDIAN	Calories per serving	Fat (Grams)	% Calories as fat
Curried Sour Chick-peas (*Khatta Chana*) Chick-peas, chili peppers, onions, tomatoes, oil, tamarind	367	14	34
Curried Mangoes (*Kachay Aam Ki Sabzi*) Mangoes, oil, molasses, honey	309	21	60
Curried Meatballs with Spinach (*Saag Keema Kofta*) Lamb, garlic, spinach, egg, oil, wheat germ, tomatoes, chili peppers	464	27	53
Curried Minced Lamb (*Keema*) Lamb, oil, onions, garlic, tomatoes, chili peppers	380	23	54
Curried Mushroom and Spinach (*Khumma/Palak Bhaji*) Mushrooms, spinach, honey, oil	135	7	49

INDIAN	Calories per serving	Fat (Grams)	% Calories as fat
Curried Mustard Leaves (*Asho Ko Rye Saag*) Mustard greens, oil, chili pepper	132	11	78
Curried Prawns with Coconut (*Jhinga Curry*) Shrimp, coconut, oil, garlic, tamarind, chili peppers	437	33	67
Curried Zucchini (*Turai Bhaji*) Zucchini, oil, tomatoes	105	9	79
Dry Chicken Curry (*Bhuni Murgi*) Chicken, oil, onions, tomatoes, yogurt	508	22	38
Fish Curry with Coconut Milk (*Machli Ka Saalan*) Fish, lentils, flour, coconut milk, oil, onions, chili peppers, garlic, tamarind, coriander seeds	500	41	73

INDIAN	Calories per serving	Fat (Grams)	% Calories as fat
Fish with Mustard Oil (*Paturi*) Fish, oil, chili peppers	241	16	59
Fruit Salad with Thickened Milk (*Phal Ka Salaad, Rabri Kay Saath*) Mangoes, apple, banana, orange, almonds, pistachios, milk, molasses	317	9	26
Gingered Cauliflower (*Asho Ko Rye Saag*) Cauliflower, oil, chili peppers	165	12	64
Kabobs of Minced Meat (*Seekh Kabab*) Beef, oil, flour, yogurt, poppy seeds	335	23	62
Kabobs with Lentils (*Shami Kabab*) Lamb, lentils, onions, eggs, flour, oil, chili peppers	415	19	41

INDIAN	Calories per serving	Fat (Grams)	% Calories as fat
Kabobs with Mangoes (*Gosht Aur Chukandar Ka Korma*) Beef, garlic, mango, onions, oil, chili peppers	149	10	57
Lamb Curry (*Rogan Josh*) Lamb, almonds, poppyseeds, coconut, garlic, oil, onions, tomatoes, yogurt, chilies	741	49	59
Lassi Yogurt, honey	88	4	43
Lentils and Vegetables with Chicken Lentils, chicken, butter, eggplant, spinach, tomatoes, onions, squash	404	13	30
Lentil Soup (*Masur Daal*) Lentils, chili peppers, onions, tomatoes, oil, butter	288	12	38

INDIAN	Calories per serving	Fat (Grams)	% Calories as fat
Lentils and Spinach (*Arhar Daal Aur Saag*) Lentils, garlic, spinach, oil, chili peppers, tamarind	157	5	29
Lentils with Vegetables (*Sambar*) Lentils, onions, eggplant, tomato, oil, coconut, chili peppers, okra, tamarind, coriander seeds	240	9	33
Mango Chutney (*Pakay Aam Ki Chutney*) Mangoes, honey	108	<1	3
Mango Fool Mangoes, honey, milk	228	6	25
Mango Ice Cream Mangoes, milk, honey, eggs, cream, arrowroot	208	14	60

INDIAN	Calories per serving	Fat (Grams)	% Calories as fat
Meat and Potato Curry (*Halka Gosht Aur Alu Ka Saalan*) Meat, onions, potatoes, tomatoes, oil, garlic	371	21	52
Meat Curry with Beets (*Gosht Aur Chukandar Ka Korma*) Beef, beets, oil, garlic	365	25	60
Meat Rolls Stuffed with Nuts (*Kaju Badaam Bharay Pasanday*) Beef, garlic, oil, onions, cashews, pistachios, coconut, yogurt, chili peppers	566	41	66
Minced Meat with Peas (*Keema Matar*) Beef, garlic, oil, onion, peas, butter, yogurt, potatoes, poppy seed	365	22	54

INDIAN	Calories per serving	Fat (Grams)	% Calories as fat
Naan (Baked Bread) Flour, eggs, milk, oil, honey, yeast, yogurt	114	3	24
Onion Salad (*Pyaz Ka Salaad*) Onions, chili peppers	36	< 1	5
Pineapple Fruit Salad (*Annanas Salaad*) Pineapple, pineapple juice, banana, raisins, pistachios, honey, apple, strawberries, sour cream, arrowroot	121	3	24
Potato Cutlets (*Alu Ki Tikki*) Potatoes, chili peppers, flour, oil	225	13	51
Rice and Chicken Pilaf (*Murgh Pullau*) Chicken, brown rice, yogurt, ginger, oil	765	24	29

INDIAN	Calories per serving	Fat (Grams)	% Calories as fat
Rice and Lamb (*Shahi Biryani*) Lamb, brown rice, oil, onions, cream, almonds, raisins, yogurt	942	56	54
Rice and Lentil Bread (*Dosa*) Brown rice, lentils, chili pepper, oil	169	6	32
Rice Cooked in Coconut Milk (*Nariyal Chaval*) Brown rice, coconut milk, oil, onions	993	70	64
Rice Pilaf with Fish (*Biryani E Mahi*) Fish, flour, butter, onions, milk, brown rice, yogurt	518	20	34
Rice Pilaf with Peas (*Matar Pullau*) Brown rice, peas, onions, oil	414	13	28

INDIAN	Calories per serving	Fat (Grams)	% Calories as fat
Rice with Chick-peas (*Chana Chaval*) Chick-peas, brown rice, chili peppers, oil, onions, ginger	416	13	27
Spiced Rice with Eggs (*Tehri*) Brown rice, eggs, oil, onions	483	19	36
Spicy Pureed Mixed Greens (*Saag*) Spinach, mustard greens, broccoli, kale, garlic, oil, onions, green pepper	175	10	52
Spicy Rice (*Masalla Pullau*) Brown rice, oil, onions	473	16	31
Spicy Stuffed Okra (*Masalla Bhari Bhindi*) Okra, oil, coriander seeds	166	14	77

INDIAN	Calories per serving	Fat (Grams)	% Calories as fat
Split Pea Soup (*Daal Ka Soup*) Split peas, tomatoes, cranberries, butter, onions, sour cream	242	9	32
Sweet and Sour Cabbage (*Khat Mithi Gobi*) Cabbage, oil, honey, almonds	119	8	64
Tandoori Chicken (*Tandoori Murgh*) Chicken, garlic, onions, oil, yogurt	207	9	38
Tomato Chutney (*Asho Ko Tamatar Chutney*) Tomatoes, oil, onions, garlic, chili peppers	148	12	72

CARIBBEAN FOOD

You probably won't find a more eclectic collection of culture and cuisine than in the Caribbean islands. The foods reflect the tastes of the various countries that have controlled and influenced the islands throughout history, including Spain, France, Denmark, the Netherlands, Africa, Britain, India, and China. Each island has its own specialties, but some dishes are just as likely to be found on the island of Jamaica as they are in French Martinique. As with the African listings, the place of origin (in this case the island) is indicated for each dish.

Though many Caribbean dishes begin with healthful, low-fat seafood, they generally also call for lots of oil and butter. The result: Almost one-half of the dishes listed in this section have 50 percent or more of their calories coming from fat. If you're creating Caribbean cuisine at home, reduce the added fat in seafood dishes and trim excess fat from the leanest cuts of meat in those recipes that call for meat. If you're in the Caribbean or at a Caribbean restaurant, your safest food choice is seafood unadulterated with rich sauces and creams. Broiled fish (about 107 calories per 4 ounces), boiled shrimp (125 calories per 4 ounces), steamed lobster (136 calories per 4 ounces) or grilled salmon (187 calories per 4 ounces) are all excellent fat-free choices. In addition, fresh fruits are usually in abundance on the islands, so take advantage while you're there.

CARIBBEAN BEST BETS

Baked Bananas Flambee • Baked Pawpaw • Black Bean Soup • Carrot Pudding with Rum Sauce • Chicken Soup • Okra with Shrimp • Red Beans and Rice • Rice with Pork • Shrimp and Rice • Stuffed Fish • Sweet Potato Cake

Caribbean	Calories per serving	Fat (Grams)	% Calories as fat
Asparagus Pudding (U.S. Virgin Islands) Asparagus, flour, milk, eggs	307	24	70
Baked Bananas Flambee (Antigua) Bananas, sugar, rum, butter	393	12	27
Baked Lobster (Jamaica) Lobster meat, butter, onions, bread crumbs	378	25	60
Baked Pawpaw (Jamaica) Papaya, butter, onion, tomatoes, bread crumbs, Parmesan cheese	347	13	35
Baked Red Snapper (*Pargo Asado,* Cuba) Snapper, oil, onions, almonds, lime juice, chili pepper	636	28	39

CARIBBEAN	Calories per serving	Fat (Grams)	% Calories as fat
Baked Snapper with Green Sauce (*Pargo Asado con Salsa Esmeralda,* Cuba) Snapper, butter, potatoes, oil, pimientos, egg yolks, almonds, lime juice	1211	80	60
Banana Bread (Jamaica) Bananas, butter, sugar, egg, flour, raisins, pecans	351	15	39
Banane Celeste (Martinique) Bananas, cream cheese, sugar, butter, cream	462	33	63
Beef Curry (Trinidad) Beef, oil, onions, coconut, milk, chili pepper	828	42	45
Beef Fillet Pot Roasted (*Filete al Caldero,* Puerto Rico) Beef, oil, onions, mushrooms	659	38	52

Caribbean	Calories per serving	Fat (Grams)	% Calories as fat
Beef with Eggplant (*Aubergines Toufes ou Toufay,* Haiti) Beef, oil, salt pork, eggplants, tomato paste, broth	1267	103	73
Beefsteak, Creole Style (*Biste a la Criolla,* Cuba) Beef, onion, butter	464	21	41
Black Bean Soup (Trinidad) Black beans, onion, pig's tail, celery, broth	190	2	9
Cabbage with Corned Beef (*Chou a Pomme avec la Viande Salee,* Martinique) Cabbage, corned beef, onions, oil, chili peppers	1057	83	71
Callalo (Trinidad) Spinach, broth, onion, salt pork, crabmeat, coconut, milk, okra	633	57	81

CARIBBEAN	Calories per serving	Fat (Grams)	% Calories as fat
Carrot Dumplings (Montserrat) Carrots, flour, butter	52	3	50
Carrot Pudding with Rum Sauce (English-speaking islands) Carrots, raisins, rum, butter, sugar, flour, eggs	520	21	36
Carry de Mouton (Martinique–Guadeloupe) Lamb, butter, onion, ham, broth, coconut milk, cream, tomatoes	631	39	56
Casseroled Beefsteak (*Bistec en Cazuela,* Puerto Rico) Beef, orange juice, lard, onions, broth	639	21	29

Caribbean	Calories per serving	Fat (Grams)	% Calories as fat
Chicken and Rice Stew	805	33	37
(*Asopao de Pollo,* Puerto Rico) Chicken, lard, onion, bell pepper, ham, tomatoes, rice, broth, peas, olives, Parmesan cheese, pimientos, asparagus			
Chicken Curry	790	51	58
(*Colombo de Poulet,* Martinique–Guadeloupe) Chicken, oil, onions, mango, pumpkin, papaya, eggplant, chayote, taro, wine			
Chicken with Lentils and Pineapple	903	38	38
(*Pollo con Lentejas y Pina,* Dominican Republic) Lentils, chicken, onion, pineapple, pineapple juice, broth			

CARIBBEAN	Calories per serving	Fat (Grams)	% Calories as fat
Chicken with Rice (*Arroz con Pollo,* Cuba, Puerto Rico, Dominican Republic) Chicken, ham, broth, olives, tomatoes, oil, garlic, bell pepper, peas	902	39	40
Chicken Soup (*Saucochi di Gallinja,* Aruba) Chicken, broth, tomatoes, onions, potatoes, sweet potatoes, squash, corn, plantain, carrots, peas	526	15	25
Coconut Bread (Trinidad) Flour, sugar, coconut, egg, evaporated milk, butter	219	9	35
Coconut Milk Sherbet (Barbados) Coconut, milk, sugar	393	27	62
Corn and Coconut Coo-Coo (Grenada) Coconut milk, cornmeal	573	41	64

CARIBBEAN	Calories per serving	Fat (Grams)	% Calories as fat
Crabs in Pepper Sauce (*Cangrefos Enchilados,* Dominican Republic) Crabmeat, oil, onion, bell pepper, chili peppers, tomatoes, tomato puree, sugar, sherry	314	14	39
Crayfish Bisque (*Bisque de Cribiches,* Martinique) Crayfish, butter, onion, coconut milk, egg yolks	311	20	59
Cream of Pumpkin Soup (Jamaica) Pumpkin, butter, onions, broth, cream	247	20	74
Deep Dish Meat Pie (St. Thomas) Beef, onion, tomatoes, butter, bell pepper, olives, flour, sherry, chili pepper	885	58	59

CARIBBEAN	Calories per serving	Fat (Grams)	% Calories as fat
Duckling with Pineapple (*Le Caneton aux Ananas,* Guadeloupe) Duckling, butter, rum, pineapple juice, broth, pineapple, arrowroot	1443	111	69
Eggplant in Coconut Cream (*Berebein na Forno,* St. Maarten) Eggplant, butter, onions, coconut cream	386	32	74
Eggplant with Tomatoes (*Aubergine a la Tomate,* Martinique) Eggplant, onion, oil, bacon, tomatoes	118	7	56
Floating Islands (Jamaica) Sugar, cream, jelly, rum	430	35	73
Kebabs (Anguilla) Beef, pineapple juice, molasses, onions, tomatoes, bell peppers, pineapple	564	26	41

CARIBBEAN	Calories per serving	Fat (Grams)	% Calories as fat
Le Calalou (Haiti) Salt pork, bacon, fish, flour, okra, spinach, broth	181	10	49
Mango Ice Cream (Jamaica) Mango, sugar, cream, lime juice	274	15	49
Marinated Beef, Dried and Fried (*Le Tassau de Boeuf,* Haiti) Beef, onions, sugar, orange juice, oil	446	22	45
Meat Salad (*Salpicon,* Cuba) Beef, chicken, potatoes, bell pepper, lettuce, onion, olives, pimientos, oil	584	47	73
Okra with Shrimp (*Molondrones con Camarones,* Dominican Republic) Shrimp, okra, butter, onion, tomatoes, sugar, rice	392	10	22

CARIBBEAN	Calories per serving	Fat (Grams)	% Calories as fat
"Old Clothes" (*Ropa Vieja,* Cuba) Beef, carrot, turnip, leek, oil, onion, bell pepper, tomatoes, pimientos	530	24	41
Pepperpot Soup (Jamaica) Beef, salt pork, spinach, kale, onions, taro, yams, okra, butter, shrimp, coconut milk	613	42	61
Planter's Cake (Jamaica) Flour, eggs, sugar, butter, rum	537	37	62
Pork Stew with Eggplant (*Daube de Porc aux Belangeres,* Martinique) Pork, flour, oil, lard, eggplant	692	39	51
Potato Curry (*Alu Talkari,* Trinidad) Potatoes, oil, mango	327	14	39

CARIBBEAN	Calories per serving	Fat (Grams)	% Calories as fat
Pumpkin Curry (*Colombo de Giraumon,* Martinique–Guadeloupe) Pumpkin, butter, oil, bacon, onion, bell pepper, tomatoes	231	18	71
Red Beans and Rice (*Congris,* Cuba) Kidney beans, oil, onions, bell pepper, tomatoes, rice	295	6	18
Red Snapper with Avocado Sauce (*Pargo con Salsa de Aguacate,* Cuba) Snapper, onion, avocados, oil, lime juice	590	23	35
Rice, Lobster, and Shrimp Stew (*Asopao de Langosta y Camarones,* Puerto Rico) Rice, shrimp, sofrito (tomato sauce), lobster, peas, broth, olives, pimientos	769	43	51

CARIBBEAN	Calories per serving	Fat (Grams)	% Calories as fat
Rice with Pork (*Arroz con Carne de Cerdo,* Dominican Republic) Pork, rice, onion, bacon, ham, lard, tomato puree, olives	702	22	29
Roast Chicken Creole Style (*Pollo Asado a la Criolla,* Puerto Rico) Chicken, orange juice, sherry, butter, oil, onion	814	46	51
Shrimp and Rice (*Arroz con Camarones,* Dominican Republic) Shrimp, oil, onion, rice, broth, tomatoes, butter	657	23	31
Shrimp Cocktail (*Coctel de Camarones,* Dominican Republic) Shrimp, oil, sugar, onion, lemon juice	464	37	72

CARIBBEAN	Calories per serving	Fat (Grams)	% Calories as fat
Shrimp Soup (*Soupa de Camarones,* Cuba) Shrimp, butter, onion, tomatoes, potatoes, milk, corn, eggs	386	20	46
Steamed Meat Patties (*Pasteles,* Puerto Rico) Pork, ham, onion, bell pepper, pimientos, olives, raisins, chick-peas, almonds, tomatoes, oil, broth, plantains, taro, milk	346	16	41
Stuffed Bananas (*Figues Bananes Fourrees,* Haiti) Bananas, butter, raisins, rum, sugar, peanuts, cherries	317	18	50

CARIBBEAN	Calories per serving	Fat (Grams)	% Calories as fat
Stuffed Cheese with Beef Filling (*Keshy Yena coe Carni,* Curacao) Cheese, beef, butter, onion, tomatoes, mushrooms, bell pepper, brandy, eggs, raisins, olives, pickles, catsup	1463	113	70
Stuffed Cheese with Shrimp Filling (*Keshy Yena coe Cabaron,* Curacao) Cheese, shrimp, butter, onion, tomatoes, bread crumbs, raisins, sweet pickles, olives, eggs	1185	83	63
Stuffed Fish (*Pescado Relleno,* Cuba) Snapper, bread crumbs, milk, eggs, onions, carrot, olive, butter	424	15	32

CARIBBEAN	Calories per serving	Fat (Grams)	% Calories as fat
Stuffed Flank Steak (*Carne Rellena,* Dominican Republic) Steak, ham, carrot, onion, eggs, oil, tomato paste, broth, chili pepper	626	31	45
Stuffed Shoulder of Pork (*L'Epaule de Porc Fourre,* Guadeloupe) Pork, rum, bread crumbs, milk, broth	1001	49	44
Sweet Potato Cake (*Gateau de Patate,* Haiti) Sweet potatoes, bananas, butter, eggs, sugar, evaporated milk, raisins, molasses	264	7	25

MOROCCAN FOOD

Though Morocco is part of the continent of Africa, its cuisine resembles more the cuisine of the Middle East than that of the other African countries. Unique combinations of spices such as turmeric, saffron, cumin, ginger, and cinnamon give the food its exotic flavors. A favorite dish, of which there are infinite varieties, is Couscous—basically a hearty souplike dish served over semolina pasta. Some couscous dishes in this section are low in fat, like the Barley Grit and Fava Bean Couscous listed below. Others, such as Couscous with Seven Vegetables, are high fat. The amount of fat in a couscous dish varies with the amount of oil and butter used, and of course with the cut of meat in meat couscous dishes. Tagine is another typical Moroccan dish (it resembles a stew) prepared with everything from fish to Swiss chard. Again, it's the added fat that generally makes these dishes high in fat. Tagine of Swiss Chard sounds like it should be low in fat, but enough oil is added so that each serving provides a fat-laden 2 tablespoons of oil.

If you're preparing these dishes at home, merely cut the amount of oil or butter in half.

MOROCCAN BEST BETS

Barley Grit and Fava Bean Couscous • Beef Stew with Chick-peas • Caraway-Flavored Soup • Chicken with Eggs, Lemons, and Olives • Fish Tagine with Tomatoes, Potatoes, and Green Peppers • Miklee • Moroccan Bread • Orange and Grated Carrot Salad • Pastry Stuffed with Almond Paste and Dipped in Honey • Sesame Seed, Almond, and Honey Cone • Sweet Carrot Salad • Sweet Steamed Rice

MOROCCAN	Calories per serving	Fat (Grams)	% Calories as fat
Barley Grit and Fava Bean Couscous (*Cheesha Sikuk*) Fava beans, barley, butter	675	24	32
Beef Stew with Chick-Peas (*Sefrina*) Beef, chick-peas, potatoes, eggs, garlic	585	19	30
Beet Salad Beets, sugar, olive oil, lemon juice	70	3	44
Berber Couscous (*Seksu Bidaoui*) Chicken, butter, tomatoes, onion, turnips, zucchini, peas, cream, couscous	815	37	41
Caraway-Flavored Soup (*Harira Karouiya*) Milk, lemon juice, flour, sugar, caraway seeds	248	8	29
Carrot Salad Carrots, garlic, olive oil, lemon juice	86	4	38

Moroccan	Calories per serving	Fat (Grams)	% Calories as fat
Chicken Kdra with Almonds and Chick-Peas (*Djej Kdra Touimiya*) Chicken, chick-peas, almonds, butter, onions, broth, parsley	601	38	57
Chicken Simmered in Smen Chicken, onion, parsley, butter, lemon juice	637	44	62
Chicken Stuffed with Rice and Raisins Chicken, rice, butter, raisins, sugar	780	49	56
Chicken Tangine with Chick-Peas (*Djej Bil Hamus*) Chick-peas, chicken, garlic, parsley, green onions, butter, raisins	646	31	44

Moroccan	Calories per serving	Fat (Grams)	% Calories as fat
Chicken with Eggs, Lemons, and Olives (*Djej Masquid Bil Beid*) Chicken, parsley, garlic, onion, butter, eggs, lemons, olives, lemon juice	1057	19	15
Chicken with Lemons and Olives Emshmel (*Djej Emshmel*) Chicken, garlic, oil, onion, olives	535	33	55
Chicken with Onions (*Djej Bisla*) Chicken, butter, onion, cumin seeds	553	39	64
Couscous with Seven Vegetables Chick-peas, lamb, chicken, couscous, butter, onions, tomatoes, carrots, turnips, zucchini, pumpkin, raisins	1106	68	56
Cucumber Salad Cucumbers, sugar, olive oil, olives	68	5	61

MOROCCAN	Calories per serving	Fat (Grams)	% Calories as fat
Date Cake (*Mescouta*) Butter, flour, eggs, sugar, dates, walnuts, raisins	350	22	55
Eel with Raisins and Onions (*Tasira*) Eel, onions, raisins, sugar, oil	625	41	59
Eggplant Salad Eggplant, tomatoes, oil	103	9	77
Eggplant Stuffed with Brains Brains, eggplant, oil, tomatoes, garlic, eggs	229	19	73
Fish Baked with Almond Paste (*Hut Benoua*) Snapper, oil, almonds, butter, sugar, onion	916	52	51
Fish Baked with Stuffed Fruit Bass, rice, almonds, sugar, butter, dates	1176	75	57

MOROCCAN	Calories per serving	Fat (Grams)	% Calories as fat
Fish Stuffed with Eggs, Onions, and Lemons Snapper, onions, oil, parsley, butter, eggs, lemons	557	36	58
Fish Tangine with Olives (*Hut Bil Zeetoon*) Fish, olives, lemon juice	430	23	47
Fish Tagine with Tomatoes, Potatoes, and Green Peppers (*Hut Tungera*) Snapper, potatoes, tomatoes, bell peppers, garlic, tomato paste, lemon juice, oil	534	15	24
Gazelles' Horns (*Kab el Ghzal*) Flour, butter, almonds, sugar	78	5	55
Harira Onion, parsley, celery, butter, lamb, lentils, tomatoes, noodles, flour	273	12	41

MOROCCAN	Calories per serving	Fat (Grams)	% Calories as fat
Lamb Tagine Layered with Okra and Tomatoes (*Tagine Macfool Bil Melokhias*) Lamb, oil, butter, onion, garlic, parsley, okra, tomatoes	617	32	47
Lamb Tagine with Fried Eggplant (*Brania*) Lamb, parsley, garlic, onion, oil, lemon juice	677	40	53
Lamb Tagine with Raisins, Almonds, and Honey (*Mrouzia*) Lamb, almonds, raisins, honey, butter	960	49	46
Miklee Flour, yeast, sugar, oil, butter, honey	94	3	33
Moroccan Bread (*Kisra* or *Khboz*) Flour, sugar, yeast, milk, sesame seeds	252	2	5

Moroccan	Calories per serving	Fat (Grams)	% Calories as fat
Moroccan Rice Pudding (*Roz Bil Hleeb*) Rice, almonds, sugar, butter, milk	267	12	41
Orange and Grated Carrot Salad Carrots, orange, lemon juice, sugar	82	<1	3
Orange, Lettuce, and Walnut Salad (*Shlada Bellecheen*) Romaine, oranges, lemon juice, sugar, walnuts	148	9	55
Pastry Stuffed with Almond Paste and Dipped in Honey (*Braewats*) Almonds, oil, sugar, flour, honey	206	7	32
Pumpkin Couscous Chick-peas, couscous, lamb, onions, butter, carrots, pumpkin, sugar, raisins	675	31	41

MOROCCAN	Calories per serving	Fat (Grams)	% Calories as fat
Puree of Fava Beans (*Byesar*) Fava beans, garlic, olive oil	211	11	47
Sesame Seed, Almond, and Honey Cone (*Sfuf*) Flour, sesame seeds, sugar, butter, almonds	488	16	30
Sliced Tomato and Onion Salad Tomatoes, onions, olive oil, parsley	144	11	69
The Snake (*M'hanncha*) Flour, butter, almonds, sugar, egg	365	28	69
Soup of Chick-Peas (*Chorba Bil Hamus*) Chick-peas, lamb, parsley, onion, tomato paste, potatoes, lemon juice	611	45	66

Moroccan	Calories per serving	Fat (Grams)	% Calories as fat
Sweet Bisteeya with Milk and Almonds (*Keneffa*) Flour, almonds, sugar, cornstarch, milk	420	16	33
Sweet Carrot Salad Carrots, garlic, olive oil, sugar, lemon juice	145	1	3
Sweet Dessert Couscous Couscous, butter, almonds, walnuts, sugar, dates	539	22	36
Sweet Steamed Rice (*Roz Mafooar*) Rice, butter, sugar	206	4	17
Tagine of Lamb with Dates Lamb, garlic, butter, onion, dates	695	30	39

MOROCCAN	Calories per serving	Fat (Grams)	% Calories as fat
Tagine of Lamb with Green Peppers and Tomatoes (*Tagine el Lahm Felfla Matisha*) Lamb, garlic, parsley, oil, tomatoes, bell peppers, lemon juice	600	31	47
Tagine of Lamb with Raisins Lamb, butter, onions, garlic, tomatoes, raisins, almonds	707	37	47
Tagine of Okra and Tomatoes (*Marak Matisha Bil Melokhias*) Okra, tomatoes, oil	138	8	50
Tagine of Swiss Chard (*Marak silk*) Chard, onion, coriander, oil, rice	319	27	76
Tomato and Green Pepper Salad Bell peppers, tomatoes, olive oil, lemon juice	78	6	66

THAI
FOOD

Thai food possesses unique flavor among the Oriental cuisines. Perhaps it's because of the frequent use of garlic, coconut milk, and small amounts of sugar. In fact, Thai recipes call for coconut milk and coconut cream more often than any other cuisine in this book. As a result of the frequent use of this high-fat ingredient, about one-half of the Thai dishes in this section provide 50 percent or more of their calories from fat. Remember that the calorie counts and the percent of calories from fat do not include rice. Cut the serving size of a main dish like a Thai curry by half, add a generous serving of white rice, and both the total calories and the percent calories from fat decrease. The Best Bets listed below provide 31 percent or less calories from fat. Don't be surprised that three of the Best Best are "fried." They are actually stir-fried with small amounts of butter or oil. Most of the coconut milk or cream-containing dishes are far worse in terms of calories and fat.

THAI BEST BETS

Corn and Shrimp Soup • *Fried Rice with Chicken* • *Mangoes and Sticky Rice* • *Papaya and Shrimp Salad* • *Plain Fried Rice* • *Shrimp and Orange Chili Salad* • *Squid Salad* • *Sweet and Sour Cucumber* • *Thai Fried Bananas*

THAI	Calories per serving	Fat (Grams)	% Calories as fat
Baked Custard Squares (*Kanom Mo Kaeng*) Coconut milk, eggs, sugar	300	20	59
Bamboo Shoots and Pork Soup (*Gaeng Chud No Mai*) Pork, bamboo shoots, onions, broth, sugar, oil, garlic, fish sauce, onions	213	12	50
Bananas in Coconut Milk (*Kluay Buat*) Bananas, coconut milk, sugar, mung beans	292	18	55
Bananas and Corn in Coconut Cream (*Kluay Lae Kaopot Buat*) Bananas, corn, sugar, coconut milk, sesame seed	326	18	46

THAI	Calories per serving	Fat (Grams)	% Calories as fat
Beef Balls in Peanut Sauce (*Panaeng Neua*) Beef, flour, oil, garlic, coconut milk, peanut butter, sugar	605	45	67
Cabbage Salad (*Yam Galumblee*) Cabbage, pork, oil, garlic, onion, peanuts, coconut milk, shrimp, fish sauce, lime juice	181	13	62
Chicken and Cabbage (*Gai Galumblee*) Chicken, coconut milk, cabbage, sugar, burdock root, fish sauce, curry paste, lime juice	444	36	73
Chicken and Coconut Milk Soup (*Gaeng Dom Yam Gai*) Coconut milk, chicken, onions, chilies, fish sauce, celery	605	54	80

THAI	Calories per serving	Fat (Grams)	% Calories as fat
Chicken in Peanut Sauce (*Gai Tua*) Chicken, garlic, curry paste, broccoli, coconut cream, onions, oil, peanut butter, sugar, coconut milk, fish sauce	351	25	64
Chicken with Chestnuts (*Gai Gup Kao Lad*) Chicken, liver, garlic, oil, broth, water chestnuts, sugar	278	13	41
Chicken with Ginger (*Gai King*) Chicken, onion, garlic, oil, mushrooms, chilies, sugar, fish sauce, ginger	170	8	42
Combination Thai Fried Rice (*Kao Pad*) Rice, pork, garlic, onions, oil, eggs, bell pepper, tomato, shrimp, chili sauce, fish sauce, cucumber	575	24	37

THAI	Calories per serving	Fat (Grams)	% Calories as fat
Corn and Shrimp Soup (*Gaeng Chud Kaopot Aun*) Broth, garlic, oil, onions, shrimp, creamed corn, egg, fish sauce	229	7	28
Fat Horses (*Ma Uon*) Pork, chicken, crab meat, garlic, sugar, coconut cream, eggs, onion, fish sauce, burdock root	409	30	65
Fried Bean Sprouts (*Pad Tua Ngork*) Pork, garlic, oil, shrimp, sugar, bean sprouts, fish sauce	179	9	47
Fried Broccoli with Shrimp (*Pak Pad Gup Gung*) Broccoli, oil, garlic, sugar, shrimp, fish sauce, oyster sauce	159	9	50

THAI	Calories per serving	Fat (Grams)	% Calories as fat
Fried Rice with Chicken (*Kao Pad Gai*) Pork, chicken, bean curd, garlic, oil, rice, egg, chilies, fish sauce,	364	12	29
Galloping Horses (*Ma Ho*) Pork, tangerines, oil, garlic, onion, sugar, peanuts, chilies	251	18	66
Green Chicken Curry (*Gaeng Keo Wan Gai*) Chicken, coconut milk, chilies, fish sauce	461	38	75
Mangoes and Sticky Rice (*Mamuang Kao Nieo*) Rice, coconut milk, sugar, mangoes, coconut cream	566	16	26

THAI	Calories per serving	Fat (Grams)	% Calories as fat
Papaya and Shrimp Salad (*Som Tam*) Lettuce, papayas, tomatoes, shrimp, peanuts, chilies, sugar, onions, fish sauce, cabbage, lime juice, sugar	169	2	13
Pickled Vegetables (*Pak Dong*) Cauliflower, cucumber, cabbage, corn, garlic, onion, oil, sesame seeds, sugar	224	19	77
Plain Fried Rice (*Kao Pad Tamada*) Rice, shrimp, garlic, oil, catsup, onions, cucumber, fish sauce	425	15	31
Pork and Chicken Stew (*Dom Kem*) Chicken, salt pork, garlic, oil, sugar, mushrooms, chilies, spinach, eggs, burdock root, soy sauce, lard, bean curd	657	56	77

192

THAI	Calories per serving	Fat (Grams)	% Calories as fat
Pork and Shrimp Mince (*Neua Tang*) Shrimp, pork, coconut milk, sugar, chilies	370	28	68
Pork Stuffed Bell Peppers (*Prik Yai Sai Moo*) Pork, onion, garlic, egg, bell peppers, oil, burdock root	241	19	70
Pork Stuffed Omelets (*Kai Yat Sai*) Pork, snow peas, tomato, oil, sugar, eggs, burdock root, fish sauce, onion	311	25	72
Rama-A-Bathing (*Pra Ram Long Song*) Spinach, coconut milk, beef, sugar, flour, chilies, onion, peanut butter, coconut cream, fish sauce, garlic	1043	82	71

THAI	Calories per serving	Fat (Grams)	% Calories as fat
Red Beef Curry (*Gaeng Ped Neua*) Beef, coconut milk, chilies, curry paste, fish sauce	645	51	71
Sauteed Greens (*Bai Gup Kao*) Greens, crab meat, oil, garlic, fish sauce	141	8	51
Shrimp and Mushroom Soup (*Gaeng Chud Gung Gup Hed*) Broth, mushrooms, garlic, oil, shrimp, burdock root, chicken, soy sauce, onions	153	7	42
Shrimp and Orange Chili Salad (*Pla Gungsod Gup Som Keo Wan*) Shrimp, oranges, garlic, sauteed greens, lime juice, fish sauce	102	1	6
Squid Salad (*Yam Pla Muek*) Squid, garlic, fish sauce	68	1	12

THAI	Calories per serving	Fat (Grams)	% Calories as fat
Steamed Coconut Custard (*Sungkaya*) Coconut milk, eggs, sugar	391	25	57
Steamed Crab (*Poo Doon*) Pork, milk, crab meat, garlic, onion, bread, egg, chilies	196	12	54
Steamed Eggs (*Kai Doon*) Eggs, onion, pork, chilies, coconut milk, soy sauce	268	20	67
Steamed Fish Curry (*Haw Mok*) Fish, coconut milk, artichokes, rice flour, egg, onion, chilies, fish sauce, oil, curry paste	458	25	49
Sweet and Sour Beef (*Neua Brio Wan*) Beef, garlic, onion, oil, cucumber, tomato, chilies, sugar, soy sauce, cornstarch	423	25	54

THAI	Calories per serving	Fat (Grams)	% Calories as fat
Sweet and Sour Cucumber (*Kwa Brio Wan*) Cucumbers, onion, sugar	41	< 1	2
Thai Fried Bananas (*Kluay Tord*) Bananas, butter, sugar	279	8	26
Water Chestnut Salad (*Yam Krachup*) Water chestnuts, pork, onion, oil, garlic, sugar, shrimp, chilies, peanut butter, fish sauce	210	10	45

VIETNAMESE FOOD

Vietnamese is second only to Japanese cuisine for its selection of low-fat dishes. Be aware, however, that Vietnamese cuisine also has many deep-fried dishes that are not listed in this book. Ingredients for Vietnamese recipes are generally simple and few in number, and serving sizes are small. Pork is frequently used, but recipes usually call for lean cuts. As with other Oriental cuisines, rice generally accompanies the meal. Coconut milk is used occasionally and little oil is added. The Best Bets below provide less than 30 percent calories from fat. There are, however, several additional low-fat dishes listed on the following pages.

VIETNAMESE BEST BETS

Banana Leaf Cake • Bean Curd Dessert • Chicken and Rice Noodles with Pork and Egg • Chicken Steamed with Ham and Chinese Cabbage • Chicken with Ginger • Chicken with Mint • Creamed Corn Chicken Soup • Lettuce Roll with Shrimp • Rice with Chicken Casserole • Steamed Fish • Vietnamese New Year Cakes

VIETNAMESE	Calories per serving	Fat (Grams)	% Calories as fat
Bamboo Shoot Omelet (*Mang Lam Cha*) Bamboo shoots, pork, garlic, eggs, oil, fish sauce	199	18	79
Banana Leaf Cake (*Banh La*) Shrimp, pork, onions, oil, garlic, flour, tapioca, fish sauce	240	8	29
Barbecued Meatballs (*Nem Nuong*) Ham, garlic, onions, sugar, pork fat, Rice Papers, rice flour, Nuoc Leo	396	22	51
Bean Curd Dessert (*Dau Hu*) Soybeans, rice flour, sugar	500	7	13
Bean Curd–Stuffed Tomato (*Ca Chua Don Dau Hu*) Tomatoes, bean curd, mushrooms, leeks, sugar, oil, rice noodles	175	8	43

Vietnamese	Calories per serving	Fat (Grams)	% Calories as fat
Bean Sprouts Fried with Shrimp and Pork (*Gia Xao Tom Thit*) Pork, shrimp, oil, onions, bean sprouts, fish sauce	140	7	43
Beef Balls (*Bo Vien*) Beef, oil, potato flour, sugar, broth, fish sauce	277	16	52
Beef Soup with Pineapple and Tomato (*Canh Ca Chua Thom Thit Bo*) Beef, pineapple, tomato, onion, oil, broth, fish sauce	93	5	51
Buddhist Monk's Soup (*Canh Kiem*) Pumpkin, potato, peanuts, mung beans, oil, bean curd, coconut milk, rice noodles	569	52	82

VIETNAMESE	Calories per serving	Fat (Grams)	% Calories as fat
Chicken and Rice Noodles with Pork and Egg (*Bun Thang*) Pork, chicken, eggs, oil, rice noodles, onions, fish sauce	347	8	21
Chicken Steamed with Ham and Chinese Cabbage (*Ga Chung Jambon*) Chicken, ham, cabbage, onions, garlic, sugar, cornstarch, broth, fish sauce	181	6	28
Chicken with Ginger (*Thit Ga Kho Gung*) Chicken, sugar, oil, garlic, fish sauce	142	4	24
Chicken with Mint (*Ga Xe Phay*) Chicken, onion, mint	55	2	26
"Cigarette Cookies" (*Banh Sen Tan*) Mung beans, sugar, flour, coconut milk	83	2	26

Vietnamese	Calories per serving	Fat (Grams)	% Calories as fat
Creamed Corn Chicken Soup (*Bap Hop Nau Ga*) Broth, chicken, creamed corn, oil, garlic, wine, egg, fish sauce	151	4	26
Fried Cabbage with Egg (*Bap Cai Xao Trung*) Cabbage, oil, garlic, egg, fish sauce	76	5	59
Fried Egg with Pork and Onion (*Cha Trung Duc Thit*) Pork, onion, oil, garlic, eggs, fish sauce	88	7	68
Fried Pork with Tomato Sauce (*Heo Ram Sot Ca*) Pork, oil, sugar, tomato paste, garlic, soy sauce, fish sauce	223	9	38
Fried Rice with Egg (*Com Chien Trung*) Egg, rice, oil, garlic	220	8	33

VIETNAMESE	Calories per serving	Fat (Grams)	% Calories as fat
Fried Rice with Shrimp and Crab (*Com Chien Thap Cam*) Shrimp, crab meat, eggs, garlic, rice, onions, oil	268	12	40
Happy Pancake (*Banh Khoai*) Flour, cornstarch, onions, pork, garlic, shrimp, bean sprouts, mushrooms, eggs, oil, fish sauce	518	32	56
Lettuce Roll with Shrimp (*Cuon Diep*) Rice noodles, shrimp, pork, lettuce, onion	190	4	18
Mimosa Rice (*Com Hoa Mimosa*) Rice, coconut milk, carrot, peas, sausage, chicken, pork, sugar, eggs, oil, garlic, onions, chicken	727	41	51

VIETNAMESE	Calories per serving	Fat (Grams)	% Calories as fat
Nuoc Leo Sauce (¹/₄ cup) Liver, pork heart, tomato paste, garlic, oil, peanut butter, sugar, sesame seeds, peanuts, soy sauce	128	9	62

Pork and Shrimp
   Simmered with Fish
   Sauce
(*Tom Thit Kho Rim*)
Pork, shrimp, sugar, oil,
onions
	178	7	34

Rice Papers (*Banh Uot*) Flour, tapioca, cornstarch, oil	54	1	23
Rice with Chicken **Casserole** (*Com Tay Cam*) Chicken, sugar, oil, garlic, onions, mushrooms, cornstarch, rice, broth	407	9	21

VIETNAMESE	Calories per serving	Fat (Grams)	% Calories as fat
Saigon Soup (*Hu Tieu*) Pork, chicken, beef, shrimp, crabmeat, celery, broth, pork heart, oil, garlic, rice noodles, peanuts, fish sauce	717	22	27
Shaking Beef (*Bo Luc Lac*) Beef, garlic, sugar, oil, onion, watercress, fish sauce	104	6	55
Sound Pancakes (*Banh Xeo*) Flour, cornstarch, coconut milk, pork, garlic, onions, shrimp, bean sprouts, mushrooms, eggs, oil, fish sauce	584	37	58
Soup with Cabbage Pork Rolls (*Canh Thit Goi Su*) Pork, cabbage, garlic, onions, rice, beef, fish sauce	405	13	28

VIETNAMESE	Calories per serving	Fat (Grams)	% Calories as fat
Steamed Fish (*Ca Hap*) Fish, sugar, mushrooms, rice noodles, pork, onions, garlic, celery, bamboo shoots, tomato	207	4	18
Stir-Fried Beef with Celery (*Ghit Bo Xao Can*) Beef, bell pepper, celery, tomato, onion, cornstarch, sugar, oil, garlic, fish sauce	96	5	50
Stuffed Chicken Necks Cooked in Coconut Milk (*Co Ga Don Thit*) Chicken necks, onions, pork, mushrooms, peas, garlic, oil, coconut milk	344	31	82
Three-Meat Vegetable Dish (*Xao Thap Cam*) Chicken, pork, beef, mushrooms, cornstarch, oil, onions, garlic, bamboo shoots, carrot, nuts, snow peas, bell pepper, fish sauce	137	7	44

VIETNAMESE	Calories per serving	Fat (Grams)	% Calories as fat
Vegetables with Meat in Grapefruit (*Nom Trai Buoi*) Pork, carrot, cucumber, shrimp, onion, bean sprouts, squid, sesame seeds, grapefruit, chili pepper	98	3	24
Vietnamese Boiled Pate (*Cha Lua*) Ham, rice flour, sugar, pork fat, fish sauce	109	10	78
Vietnamese Boneless Stuffed Chicken (*Ga Rut Xuong Nhoi*) Chicken, garlic, onion, sugar, fish sauce	164	5	29
Vietnamese New Year Cakes (*Banh Chung*) Mung beans, rice, onions, pork	561	11	17

VIETNAMESE	Calories per serving	Fat (Grams)	% Calories as fat
Vietnamese Roast Beef with Ginger Sauce (*Be Thui*) Beef, rice flour, onions, sugar, chili pepper, garlic, soy sauce	259	8	27

AFRICAN
FOOD

The continent of Africa is made of many countries. The diversity of Africa's nations is reflected in its cuisines, from curried dishes to chicken and peanut butter combinations. In this chapter, the country or region of origin of each dish is identified. One consistent theme of African cooking is simplicity. Most of the African recipes analyzed for this book require few ingredients and little cooking skill—good news for the novice. Also good news is that low-fat, high-fiber vegetables are the main ingredients of many recipes, making it easy to keep the fat and calories to a minimum, especially when you're preparing African food at home. Flexibility is also evident in African cooking. For many recipes, alternative vegetables or seasonings are suggested if you don't have the ones the recipe calls for. Moreover, fat- and cholesterol-laden meats are frequently absent or present only as a minor ingredient in many African dishes.

One high-fat ingredient to watch out for, however, is coconut milk. It is an essential ingredient in several African dishes. And at 552 calories and 57 grams of fat per cup, it's one to avoid.

Soups are, for the most part, a good bet. Several low-fat soups are listed below.

AFRICAN BEST BETS

Bananas with Green Split Peas • Black-eyed Peas • Cucumber and Yogurt Salad • Dumpling • Fish with Pepper Sauce • Green Bean Stew • Grilled Plantain • Pickled Fish • Pinto Beans with Potatoes • Rice and Lentils • Shrimp Soup • Squash Soup • Vegetarian Lentils • Yellow Rice

AFRICAN	Calories per serving	Fat (Grams)	% Calories as fat
Avocado with Smoked Fish (Ghana) Smoked fish, eggs, milk, sugar, oil, ripe avocados, bell pepper, lime juice	1214	109	81
Baked Curried Fish (*Mtuzi wa Samaki,* Kenya) Fish, onions, oil, tomatoes, garlic	595	26	39
Bananas with Green Split Peas (Rwanda) Split peas, bananas, oil, onion	190	5	22
Beans with Coconut Milk (Tanzania) Chick-peas, coconut milk, tomato, garlic	219	14	58
Beans with Shredded Coconut (Tanzania) Chick-peas, potatoes, oil, coconut, garlic	273	19	61

African	Calories per serving	Fat (Grams)	% Calories as fat
Black-eyed Peas (*Oshingali,* Namibia) Black-eyed peas, chili peppers	179	1	7
Buttermilk Rusks (*Karringmelkbeskuit,* South Africa) Flour, sugar, butter, egg, buttermilk	218	12	48
Chicken Curry (*Kalya e Khaas,* Southern Africa) Chicken, yogurt, tomatoes, green chilies, onions, butter, oil	880	58	59
Chickennat (Uganda) Chicken, butter, onions, broth, peanut butter, eggs	755	58	69
Chicken Peanut Stew (*Mafe,* Senegal) Chicken, oil, onions, tomatoes, tomato paste, peanut butter, cabbage, potatoes, carrots, turnips, okra	841	54	58

AFRICAN	Calories per serving	Fat (Grams)	% Calories as fat
Chicken Stew (*Doro Wat,* Ethiopia) Chicken, butter, onion, garlic, tomato paste, eggs	749	58	69
Coconut Corn Curry (East Africa) Corn, sesame seed, poppy seed, peanuts, coconut, coconut milk, butter	876	78	80
Coconut-Peanut Pumpkin (*Futari,* Tanzania) Pumpkin, sweet potatoes, onions, butter, coconut milk	149	10	60
Coconut Shrimp (*Camarao de Coco,* Mozambique) Shrimp, butter, garlic, onion, tomatoes, coconut milk	586	35	54
Combo Flatcake (Tanzania) Beef, potatoes, carrots, flour, sugar, milk, egg, oil	187	9	44

AFRICAN	Calories per serving	Fat (Grams)	% Calories as fat
Coriander Chicken (*Djedj b'l-qasbour,* Algeria) Chicken, butter, oil, garlic, olives	422	29	61
Crunchy Spice Bits [1 cup] (*Dabo Kolo,* Ethiopia) Flour, sugar, oil	359	14	35
Cucumber and Yogurt Salad (*Raita,* South Africa) Cucumbers, yogurt	59	1	18
Dumpling (*Ujeqe,* South Africa) Flour, cornmeal, butter, milk, eggs	399	10	22
Fish Soup (*Caldo de Peixe,* Cape Verde) Fish, bananas, onion, oil, garlic, tomatoes, tapioca, potatoes, bread crumbs, cabbage	473	10	18

African	Calories per serving	Fat (Grams)	% Calories as fat
Fish with Pepper Sauce (Ghana) Fish, tomatoes, onions, chili pepper	227	10	32
Fried Cabbage (Tanzania) Cabbage, oil, tomato, carrots, bell pepper	128	12	84
Greens (*Masamba,* Malawi) Turnip greens, tomatoes, peanut powder, onions	85	4	42
Greens and Peanuts (*Um'Bido,* South Africa) Spinach, peanuts, butter	224	16	65
Green Beans in Lamb Sauce (*Loubya Khadra Marqa,* Algeria) Lamb, olive oil, onions, tomatoes, green beans	251	16	56

AFRICAN	Calories per serving	Fat (Grams)	% Calories as fat
Green Bean Stew (Green Bean *Bredie,* South Africa) Green beans, onions, mutton, oil, sugar, potatoes	572	19	29
Green Pea Soup (Southern Africa) Split peas, onion, butter, garlic	203	8	33
Grilled Plantain (Togo) Plantains	174	< 1	2
Groundnut Stew (*Hkatenkwan,* Ghana) Chicken, onion, tomato paste, oil, tomatoes, peanut butter, eggplant, okra	618	39	57
Jollof Rice (Mali) Rice, tomatoes, tomato paste, onions, oil, garlic, lamb	546	25	41

AFRICAN	Calories per serving	Fat (Grams)	% Calories as fat
Kentumere (Ghana) Oil, onions, tomatoes, kippered herring, spinach	581	59	92
Lamb and Rice (*Skudahkharis,* Somalia) Lamb, oil, onion, tomatoes, garlic, tomato paste, rice	791	38	44
Lamb Chunks on Skewers (*Sosaties,* Southern Africa) Lamb, garlic, oil, onions, sugar, jam, flour	524	21	36
Lentil Soup (*Chorba 'dess,* Algeria) Lentils, veal, olive oil, carrot, potato, onion	293	12	36
Mango Snow (Tanzania) Mangoes, sugar	105	< 1	3

AFRICAN	Calories per serving	Fat (Grams)	% Calories as fat
Meat with Rice and Lentils (*Biryani,* South Africa) Beef, yogurt, butter, rice, lentils, eggs, garlic, onion	696	39	50
Palm Nut Soup (*Abenkwan,* Ghana) Palm oil, onions, tomatoes, okra, eggplant, fish	1152	112	88
Peanut Butter Stew (*Dovi,* Zimbabwe) Chicken, peanut butter, onions, butter, garlic, bell peppers, spinach	539	34	56
Pickled Fish (*Ingelegde Vis,* South Africa) Fish, onions, sugar	243	6	23
Pinto Beans with Potatoes (Rwanda) Pinto beans, potatoes, celery, oil	210	8	35

African	Calories per serving	Fat (Grams)	% Calories as fat
Plantains in Coconut Milk (Kenya) Plantains, coconut milk	318	18	50
Pumpkin Stew (Pumpkin *Bredie,* South Africa) Pumpkin, lamb, oil, onions, sugar	502	20	36
Red Beet Salad (*Rooibeet Slaai,* South Africa) Beets, onions, sugar	20	< 1	3
Rice and Lentils (*Koushry,* Egypt) Lentils, rice, onions, oil	334	6	16
Sardines in Tomato Sauce (Benin) Sardines, onion, garlic, oil, tomatoes, spinach	178	9	44
Shrimp Soup (*Caldo de Camarao,* Cape Verde) Shrimp, bananas, onion, olive oil, garlic, tomatoes, potatoes	379	7	15

AFRICAN	Calories per serving	Fat (Grams)	% Calories as fat
Spiced Red Beans in Coconut Milk (*Maharagwe,* Kenya) Kidney beans, onions, oil, tomatoes, coconut milk	325	22	61
Spicy Vegetable Soup (*Chorba Hamra,* Algeria) Lamb, butter, onion, tomatoes, potato, carrot, zucchini, celery, chick-peas, vermicelli	380	22	53
Spinach Stew (Central African Republic) Spinach, bell pepper, onions, oil, tomatoes, peanut butter	156	10	60
Squash Soup (Mozambique) Squash, garlic, onion, butter	50	2	27

AFRICAN	Calories per serving	Fat (Grams)	% Calories as fat
Stuffed Crabs (*Akotonshi,* Ghana) Crabmeat, oil, onion, tomatoes, bell peppers, tomato paste, egg, bread crumbs, garlic	258	12	42
Tomato Stew (Tomato *Bredie,* South Africa) Lamb, tomatoes, onions, oil, sugar, garlic	443	19	38
Vegetable Mafe (Senegal) Onions, oil, pumpkin, turnips, potatoes, carrots, cabbage, tomatoes, spinach, tomato sauce, peanut butter	429	22	47
Vegetarian Lentils (South Africa) Lentils, oil, onion, tomatoes, garlic	258	8	27
Yellow Rice (South Africa) Rice, butter, raisins	434	10	20

AFRICAN	Calories per serving	Fat (Grams)	% Calories as fat
Zucchini with Peanuts (Chad) Zucchini, peanuts, butter	230	19	68

REFERENCES

Africa News Service, Inc. *The African News Cookbook*. New York: Viking Penguin, 1986.

Andoh, Elizabeth. *At Home with Japanese Cooking*. New York: Alfred A. Knopf, 1980.

Brennan, Jennifer. *The Original Thai Cookbook*. New York: Richard Marek Publishers, 1981.

Brennan, Jennifer. *The Cuisines of Asia*. New York: St. Martin's/Marek, 1984.

Chantiles Liacouras, Vilma. *The Food of Greece*. New York: Atheneum, 1975.

Child, Julia and Simone Beck. *Mastering the Art of French Cooking, Volume Two*. New York: Alfred A. Knopf, 1983.

Childress, Marjorie and Clyde Childress. *Adventures in Mexican Cooking*. San Francisco: Ortho Books, 1978.

Froud, Nina. *The International Jewish Cook Book*. New York: Stein and Day Publishers, 1978.

223

Greek Orthodox Ladies Philoptochos Society. *Popular Greek Recipes*. Charleston, SC: Charleston Lithographing Company, 1976.

Greer, Lindsay Ann. *Creative Mexican Cooking*. Austin, Texas: Texas Monthly Press, 1985.

Hazan, Marcella. *The Classic Italian Cookbook*. New York: Alfred A. Knopf, 1976.

Kennedy, Diana. *The Cuisines of Mexico*. New York: Harper & Row, 1972.

Mehta, Shahnaz with Joan Bravo Korenblit. *Good Cooking From India*. New York: Gramercy Publishing Company, 1985.

Myers, Barbara. *The Chinese Restaurant Cookbook*. Briarcliff Manor, NY: Stein and Day Publishers, 1982.

Ngo, Bach and Gloria Zimmerman. *The Classic Cuisine of Vietnam*. Woodbury, NY: Barron's, 1979.

Ortiz Lambert, Elisabeth. *The Complete Book of Caribbean Cooking*. New York: Ballantine Books, 1986.

Prudhomme, Paul. *The Prudhomme Family Cookbook*. New York: William Morrow and Company, 1987.

Rose, Evelyn. *The Complete International Jewish Cookbook*. London: Robson Books, 1984.

Schuler, Elizabeth. *German Cookery*. New York: Crown Publishers, 1978.

Thayer, Leung and Yuk Mai. *The Classic Chinese Cook Book*. New York: Harper & Row, 1987.

Wolfer, Paula. *Couscous and Other Good Food From Morocco*. New York: Harper & Row, 1987.